The Part-Time Trader

Founded in 1807, John Wiley & Sons is the oldest independent publishing company in the United States. With offices in North America, Europe, Australia and Asia, Wiley is globally committed to developing and marketing print and electronic products and services for our customers' professional and personal knowledge and understanding.

The Wiley Trading series features books by traders who have survived the market's ever changing temperament and have prospered—some by reinventing systems, others by getting back to basics. Whether a novice trader, professional or somewhere in-between, these books will provide the advice and strategies needed to prosper today and well into the future.

For a list of available titles, visit our Web site at www.WileyFinance.com.

The Part-Time Trader

Ryan Mallory

WILEY

Cover image: © Alamy/BigshotD3
Cover design: Wiley

Published by John Wiley & Sons, Inc., Hoboken, New Jersey.
Published simultaneously in Canada.

For general information on our other products and services or for technical support, please contact our Customer Care Department within the United States at (800) 762-2974, outside the United States at (317) 572-3993 or fax (317) 572-4002.

Wiley publishes in a variety of print and electronic formats and by print-on-demand. Some material included with standard print versions of this book may not be included in e-books or in print-on-demand. If this book refers to media such as a CD or DVD that is not included in the version you purchased, you may download this material at http://booksupport.wiley.com. For more information about Wiley products, visit www.wiley.com.

ISBN 9781118650059 (Hardcover)
ISBN 9781118650080 (ePDF)
ISBN 9781118650042 (ePub)

Printed in the United States of America
10 9 8 7 6 5 4 3 2 1

To my wonderful wife, Keenan Mallory, who has been by my side every step of the way, and for Jason, the wonderful son she gave me, who has been our greatest accomplishment in this life together.

CONTENTS

Acknowledgments xvii

PART I **THE BASICS FOR PART-TIME TRADING** **1**

CHAPTER 1 **So How Much Do You Really Hate Your Job?** **3**

Becoming Determined to Find a Way Out 4
Shorting My Own Career 5
It Was Not in Real Estate 5
It Started to Unravel 5
Stocks Would Be a Much Better Option for Me 6
I Loved Trading but Hated My Job—Something Had to Give 7
Corporate Hierarchy 7
Those at the Top 7
Those Who Wish They Were 7
As Harmless as the Swiss 8
The Malcontents 9
Guilty as Charged 9
An Inward Reflection 10
Not an Easy Road to Take 10
Realize You Still Need Your Job 11
Professional Paper Pushers 12
Too Many Cookies 13

E-mail Paranoia 13
Finding the Escape Hatch 14
Corporate Depression 14

CHAPTER 2 How Did I Become a Full-Time Trader? 17

My Trading Foundation 18
Rudimentary Understanding of Risk 18
A New Trading World 19
Turning against Investing 19
Open-Minded to Becoming a Trader 21
Road Bumps Ahead 22
Keeping Tabs in an Awkward Kind of Way 22
Leaving Penny Stocks Behind 24
In Search of a Shortcut 24
False Hopes in Books 25
My Experience with Trading at Work 26
Accepting the Cards I Was Dealt 26
Flying Undected 27
Don't Obsess Over Profits 29
More Money Than I Could Afford to Lose 29
A Fresh Dose of Market Reality 30
A Learning Experience, Indeed 31
Understanding Risk Aversion 32
A Simple Step for Controlling the Emotions 32

CHAPTER 3 Where Wall Street Meets the Office 35

Work Ambivalence 36
Nonsensical Reports 36
Workplace Scalawag 37
Decide How Successful You Want to Be at Your Job 38
The Boss Man Reviews 39
Creating a Friendly Coalition 39
The Approach 40
The Good Samaritan 40
Peer Kindness 41
Reaping What You Sow 41

Filling Out Your Own Review 41
Don't Be Modest 42
In the Boss Man's Hands 43
Seeking Out Increased Responsibility versus Effective Trading 44
More Work = Difficult Trading 44
Work Never Gets Back to Normal 45
Promotion Competition 45
Broad-Based Mindset 45
Endless Competition 46
Finding a Way Despite the Adversity 46
The Job Is a Trading Asset 47

CHAPTER 4 Don't Quit Your Day Job ... SERIOUSLY! 49

Just Like the "Real World" 50
Making Everyone Happy 51
Managing the Two 52
Avoid Goals That Give You a False Sense of Hope 52
The Unstoppable Trader 53
Losing All Logic 53
Not a Chance 54
Mind-Numbing Trading 56
Real-World Fantasies 56
Spreadsheet Trade Management 57
Don't Watch the Benjamins 57
The Squeeze 58
More Money, More Problems 58
Focus on the Trade Only 59
The Right Position Sizes 60
Position Sizes Dictate Emotional Depth 60
Why Don't We All Just Trade as Big as We Can? 61
What Do We Do Then? 61
What Should I Do? 61
Jeopardize Your Trade Before You Jeopardize Your Job 62
Job Is Priority Number One 63
Three Parameters to Account For 63

CHAPTER 5 **The Essentials to Your "Workplace Trading Desk"** 65

Environmental Trading 65
Office Squares 66
Go Small 66
How to Lay Out Your Office 67
Working with the Computer that You Are Given 71
Desktop versus Laptop 72
Filling Out the Request Form 73
The Laptop Luxury 73
Getting Through Meetings 74
Additional Advantages 75
Stuck with the Desktop 75
Making What You Have Better 75
Web-Based Trading 76
Using Your Smartphones and Tablets as Trading Tools 77
Social Media and Workplace Trading 77

PART II **THE GAME PLAN** 79

CHAPTER 6 **Before You Clock In** 81

Your Research Must Be Done 81
A Typical Morning 82
Start-Time Struggles 82
Running Late 83
Parking Is Not as Easy as It Looks 83
Office Routes 84
Printer Friendly 85
Prideful Management 86
Delayed E-mails 86
Leave the Lights On 87
Beating the Light Sensors 87
Being Concise and Actionable with Your Research 88
Market Analysis 88
Stay Clear of the Dow 89
Knowing Your Trade Setups 89
Illegible to Others 89
Time-Zone Trading 90
Avoid the Clutter 91

Trade Your Plan 91
Your Strategy for the Day Should Be Tailored around Your Workload 92
Don't Go for the Easy Way Out 93
Avoid "Prop Firms" 93

CHAPTER 7 Your Best Friend Is the Person Who Works in IT 95

Know How Your IT Department Works 95
Small Companies 96
Harder to Blend In 96
Just Do a Good Job 96
Large Companies 97
Too Big to Notice Initially 97
Indiscriminate Toward Individual Performance 97
Which One Is Better? 98
One Way to Turn the Tables 99
Ideally, Get to Know Someone from That Department 99
You Only Need One 99
Do Not Be Turned Off by Their Standoffishness 99
A Friendly Conversation Ensues 100
Start Digging In 101
What You May Find Out 102
Workplace Armageddon 102
From Noble to Idiotic 103
Time for Plan B: The Boss Man's Office 103
Losing Hope 104
Caution at Every Corner 104
Understanding Their Policies and Designing Your Trading Around Them 105
Working Your Way Around Obstacles 105
Saving Tips 105
Search Out the Guest Connection 106
Keeping Your Phone to Yourself 106
Don't Call Me Maybe 107
Trying to Buy Me Off 107
Installing Company Apps 108
Some Final Thoughts 108

CHAPTER 8 **Flying Below the Radar** 111

Do Not Become a Distraction 111
Do Not Be a Clicker 112
The Mouse Click Alternative 112
Lowering the Bar 113
Workplace Peeping-Toms 114
Squatter's Rights 114
Avoid Telling Anyone that You Are a Trader 114
More Importantly, Do Not Involve Others 115
Low-Beta Stress 115
No Stocks for You! 116
Keep Things Business as Usual 117
Mild Man Trader 118
The Contrarian Indicator 118
Buy, Buy, Buy! 119
Funny Stories with a Serious Undertone 119
Now, Most Importantly 119
Do Not Spike the Ball 120

CHAPTER 9 **Adding a Passive Income to Your Day Job** 123

It's a Supplement—Not the Main Source 123
Combining the Day Job with Part-Time Trading 124
Become Systematic in Your Trading 124
Trading Should Be Natural to You 124
The "Main Thing" 125
That's Who I Am 125
Chart Types 125
Trend Following the Markets 126
Only Price and Volume 126
Bollinger Bands Are Legit 127
Limited Use for Other Purposes 128
Being Cognizant of Risk and Reward 128
The Risk in My Stops 128
Time Element 129
Successful Trading Requires You to Wait 130
Embrace the Fact that You Will Lose 130
Capital Inventory Turnover 130
Aim Small, Miss Small 131

Hit Singles and Doubles—Not Home Runs 131
Reach Base When Trading 132
Trade with What the Market Pitches You 132
Ask Yourself This ... 133

CHAPTER 10 The Best Way to Trade at Work 135

Always Use Stop-Losses 135
Stop-Loss Frustrations 135
Avoid Hindsight 136
Suck It Up 136
Use Position Sizes that Won't Be Distracting to You 137
Future Distractions 137
Priorities Became Jumbled 138
Good System, Bad Environment 139
The SharePlanner Investment System 140
Designed for Simplicity and Duplicity 140
Works Around Your Job 140
Plan Your Trade and Trade Your Plan 141
More About the Management, Not the Stock 141
Not About the Stock 142
Count the Dollars Later 142
Expecting the Worse 142
The 90/10 Rule 143
Above All Else ... Manage 144
The Door and Its Hinges 145

PART III Becoming the Part-Time Trader 147

CHAPTER 11 Trading Habits You Will Want to Avoid 149

Learning from My Shortcomings 149
Seek Improvement, Not Solutions 150
Traders and Athletes Alike 150
No Quick Fix in Trading 151
Stay Away from Trades that Force You to Dip into Margin 151
Avoid Catastrophes 152
Leveraging Has Much More Downside to It 152
An Emotional Spasm 153
Speeding Up the Process 153

Pitfalls Out of the Gate 153
Panic Ensues 154
Adding Insult to Injury 155
Do Not Do It for the Money 155
For the Love of the Game 155
Your Heart Has to Be in It 156
Winning Trades Turning into Losers—
The Ultimate Performance Killer 157
Protect the Gains 157
Small Gains Are Equally Important 158
Avoid Trading Heavily in Penny Stocks 158
Road Bumps Ahead 159

CHAPTER 12 You Still Have to Get Your Real Work Done 161

Emotions on the Job 161
Find a Middle Ground 162
Planning Around Meetings 162
Meeting Distraction 162
Blocking Out Time 163
Give No Option 163
Sneaking Out of Meetings 164
Considering Extreme Measures 164
Calling In as Much as You Can 165
Bailing Out 165
Avoid the Screen Share 166
How to Trade When Traveling 166
You Can Still Trade 167
West Coast Trading 167
Adding New Positions Prior to Travel 168
Using the Travel Time 168
Using Your Workload to
Your Trading Benefit 169
A "Debbie" in the Making 169

CHAPTER 13 What to Say and Do if Trading Becomes a Distraction 171

What You Must Avoid at All Costs 172
How to Deal with Those Who Are Far Too Curious 173
Don't Drop Your Guard 173

Getting Coworkers Off Your Scent 174
Stay Neutral 174
When Trouble Occurs 175
Matters Become Out of Control 175
Bad Turns Worse 175
Stay the Course 176
Could Have Been Worse 177
I Could Have Done Better 177
Stay "Cool" 178
When Boss-Man Comes A-knockin' 178
Problems with Day Trading 179
Swing Trading to the Outside Person 180

CHAPTER 14 More of My Personal Tricks of the Trade 181

Image and Performance 182
Everything Has to Align Together 182
Learning to Do Two Things at Once 183
I'll Second That 183
Don't Do Research at Work 184
Network Tricks 184
Be Our Guest 184
Bandwidth Red Flags 185
Rely on Handheld Technologies for Streaming 185
Scaling In and Out of Positions 186
A Simple Breakdown 186
Scaling Out of Profits 187
Scaling Long in a Falling Stock 187
Don't Be Too Social 188
No Seats Here 188
No Snacks, Either 188
Spread the Papers 189
It Is a Tricky Way of Life 190

CHAPTER 15 Take This Job and Shove It 193

How Did I Know It Was Time? 193
I Had Arrived 193
When I Finally Left 194
Build Your Own 194

Get Some Power 195
Multiple Monitors and Video Cards 195
Breaking Free 196
Life without Work Benefits 196
Why Did I Do It? 197
Providing Transparency and Honesty 197
Premium Services 198
How You Can Know if It Is Time to Leave Your 9-to-5 198
No Right Time 198
Don't Base It on Inherited Money 199
How It Affects Others 199
Exactly What Are We Talking About? 200
The Journey and Not the Destination 200
Just Being a Part-Time Trader 201
Turning It On 201
Self-Revelation 201
Let's Do It! 202

About the Author 203
About the Companion Website 205
Index 207

ACKNOWLEDGMENTS

It would be foolish of me to think that I could write this book all on my own without acknowledging those along the way who have helped bring me to this point in my life and supported me in writing this book for well over a year now as well as the support that I have received well before then that led up to this opportunity.

First, I am thankful to my beautiful wife, Keenan Mallory, who has lovingly supported me in this long journey that comes with writing a book, and stuck through it with me until the very end. She understood the late nights and early mornings, and always made sure that I was taken care of in the process.

I am also thankful to my son, Jason Mallory, who has been a light in my life that goes beyond the realm of trading and gives a meaning to life that cannot be comprehended. Hopefully, he will find my book just as riveting as all of the children's stories he has been read each night.

I would be remiss if a huge heartfelt amount of gratitude was not sent to my parents, Duane and Linda Mallory, for their years of dedication and determination, the example they have modeled for me in life, and supported, though apprehensively at times, my unorthodox adventures, and making sure that I had the best upbringing a son could ask for.

My sister, Tracy Rodgers, despite being 14 years my senior, has been a terrific example and role model for me, and a great person to talk to late at night when the rest of the world was fast asleep.

My brother, Duane, whom we also simply referred to as "Brother" over the years, has been a best friend to me and a person to ping ideas off on and encouraged me in some of life's greatest challenges and leaps of faith, including becoming a full-time trader.

Not a day goes by that I do not wish my other sibling, Jason Mallory, could be around for a five-minute conversation to tell him about all the adventures life has taken me on and perhaps he could have even joined me on some of them. He was the best friend a man could ask for and someone I always wanted to emulate.

Over the years I have been blessed to see my extended family grow as well, and though I didn't dedicate the book to them, as they would all have liked, I do hope they realize that they mean the world to me: Shelby Rodgers and Jessica, Luke, and Danielle Mallory. I am grateful to call each of them family and see them grow up through the years into some wonderful kiddos.

Close friends play a huge role in life, and I am thankful for people like Mark Billman, who has been there for me countless hours into the early morning helping me fix my computer, servers, networks, software issues, and anything technical; he has had a role in making it right for me.

I'm also grateful to my cofounder of SharePlanner.com, Matt Walters, who has help me grow the business over the past seven years into a company that has helped countless traders realize their dreams of full-time trading. And Matt's brother, Nate, through constant reminding, helped me acknowledge in my formative trading years that long-term investing was no longer the path for me to go down.

As a first time author, I am incredibly thankful for the opportunity that John Wiley & Sons has given me to put my pen to paper and have my writing made public to the world. A book lasts the test of time, and I am incredibly grateful to Laura Walsh for reaching out to me and encouraging me to write a book and for putting her backing and support behind me during the whole process. I also could not have done it without the editing team of Judy Howarth and Tula Batanchiev, who coached me throughout the process and made sense of my ramblings throughout the book.

And, of course, all things in life, including the blessing listed on these pages, would not be possible were it not for my merciful Savior in Jesus Christ, who washed away my sins of past and present and accepts me as His own.

Introduction

Sitting behind a fake mahogany desk in a chair I believe was made from some form of polyester, and staring at the walls of a musty, windowless office, I had just about all I could take. I had been a part of Corporate America for the past eight years and at a job where, if I stayed there much longer, my biggest fear may in fact become a reality—becoming a "career man" doing a job I could not be any less passionate about, just to pay the bills and support my family. Had it come to that, I may in fact have ended up in a place where I was chained to a bed surrounded by people in white coats.

Time for Boldness

That is when I knew I had to quit my job and became a full-time trader and blogger at the site I founded, SharePlanner.com. But getting to this point was not something that happened overnight. No, waiting for this dream to come to fruition probably created more anxiety inside of me than doing what I had only dreamed of doing in my mind: giving my two-week notice.

The night before, I had typed my letter of resignation. This was something that I did not have a lot of experience at, so I decided the best course of action was to google the search term *two-week notice* and simply copy what someone else had done, which might have been a bit impersonal, but come on—how personal do you really want to be with the company that you are notifying you have no desire to work at any longer? There was no turning back at this point. I was certain I would do this, though I probably was at the point where even if a fresh dose of reasoning against the decision I had set out to make came my way, it would have been pushed aside. I was determined, nervous, but set in the decision I was going to make.

My wife could not have been more nervous about the decision, and my reasons for doing so probably made no sense to anyone but myself. Of course, I did not want to burn any bridges because I was not entirely sure if what I was planning on doing in my post-corporate career would actually work out in the long term, and just maybe I would have to take the long walk of shame and ask for my old job back. So despite having a deep, deep hatred for my line of work, I had to be respectful and try not to burn any bridges in the process.

This Is It! Don't Get Scared Now

The time had come. I pumped myself up and re-read the letter of resignation for probably the 73rd time just to make sure it said what it was supposed to say, as if it would make a difference after I verbally told the boss man that I was quitting my job. There was also a hint of humor in doing that, since I really did not bother to take the time and put my own thoughts into the words that were on the two-week notice.

I got out of that itchy, synthetic polyester office chair and walked unsurely into his office, where his administrator (I guess that was the politically correct version of secretary) sat. Now this lady had it out for me. It was almost like she was spending all her hours building some grand case for why I should be fired, for reasons unbeknownst to me. She had no idea, but whatever her motivation was for constantly trying to throw a stick in my wheel spoke, her plans were just about to be set on fire and go up in smoke.

I asked her for the boss man, but he was not there. "DARN IT!" All that effort to build up the courage and walk into the office and make my intentions known was for naught. I would have to repeat the process again in two hours when he was back in his office.

Same Song, Second Verse Once he came back, the process of being bold and walking down the hallway and into the boss man's office had become easier. I started off by making some small talk with him in my pointless attempt to put off the inevitable. While I had imagined how it would all play out many times in the past, I simply found it rather difficult to put it into reality.

Finally, though, I found the courage to move on to the matter at hand and tell him that I was giving my "two-week notice."

The silence was deafening. I am pretty certain that, despite it being early in the morning, the crickets outside had found a way to voice the awkwardness of the moment.

"What are they offering you?" he asked.
"Who's offering me what?" I said confused.
"The company you are going to."
"Nothing," I said squeamishly.
"What company is it?"
"There is no company."
"Your job title?" he asked.
"Trader and blogger," I mumbled.
"Did you say what I think you said?" he asked sarcastically.
"Yes, sir," I said, with a bit of forced respect.
"Obviously, you're not leaving for the money," he concluded.

And that was the gist of our conversation. We made some additional small talk thereafter, and of course the admin in the next office over could hear it all and at times I might have even elevated my voice so that she would no doubt know what was going on. You might have thought she was going to go into cardiac arrest by the gasp she made when I made my intentions known to management.

Her simmering contempt for me would simply have to stay with herself—I was leaving on my own terms, and because I wanted to.

■ Move On

I was a short-timer who was ready for the gates to open and release him into the outside world.

Now that the cat was out of the bag, everyone knew for the first time that I was a trader. They also knew I owned a web site called SharePlanner.com. The conversations with coworkers that evolved from that point forward ranged from jealousy to admiration and curiosity to hatred.

In the eyes of many in the office, I had essentially engaged in an act of high treason against the company that put food on our table for so many years. By giving my two-week notice, I had essentially told them that I didn't need their paycheck and it wasn't because I was getting paid more somewhere else. The message that was conveyed to them was that "I don't want to do this anymore—I found something better to do."

Coworker Backlash

That didn't bode well with the kids on the playground. Over the next two weeks, everyone in the department tried to dump on me as much work as possible. But once the last week rolled around, I simply didn't care anymore. I would have these people in a near feverish panic asking me when I would get to a certain assignment, but my only response was, "Next week." That definitely irked some, but the notion that I could somehow get months' worth of assignments done, so that they would not have to be responsible for it after I left, was not possible, and as the short-timer, I was ready to be released back into society.

Some took their argument to the boss man with requests that he focus entirely on their work and corner my remaining time in the organization on their needs and wants. There was even one person who tried to stand in the doorway until I verbally submitted to her every need and want.

There were actually a few people, though, who just wanted to talk to me more about the stock market and which stock I thought might be the "next Apple." Suddenly, the old-timers on the verge of retirement wanted me to help them with portfolio allocation, and advice on various interest bearing assets. The problem was that I was just a simple trader, not a financial adviser. However, talking with them about the financial market was highly enjoyable, and being able to open up with them about what I was actually really good at, for the first time ever, was a special moment for me.

Curious Management

Then came the meeting that I had with upper management about reasons unrelated to my departure. I remember sitting in a meeting with a bunch of those "higher-ups," and they all had to give me their opinion on the lunacy that I was engaged in. Apparently, there should be no other company that I would want to work for but the one that was home to the office chair that I had parked my derriere in for years on end.

I think for them my move was even harder because here was a kid in his 20s who, in a matter of days, would not have to answer for anything to those who had controlled a large portion of his life for so long. One told me how it was a "bear market" and a horrible time to be trading, and another made me sit through his stories as a full-time day-trader that capitulated in 2000 as a result of the "dot-com" bubble.

In fact, on the last day, the admin that I told you about earlier, who had this mysterious hatred for me, reported me to Human Resources for being 15 minutes late to work on my last two days on the job.

You got me there! Guilty as charged. Directors, vice president, my immediate boss, and Human Resources were e-mailed to let them know how essentially I had not taken my job seriously on the final two days on the job, and that the company should not pay me for that time.

To make things right, I made sure I left 45 minutes early on my last day and into the world of full-time trading.

No longer would I have that biweekly paycheck to support me and my family. Trading was no longer a side job that I had become really good at.

Sharing My Secrets

For years now countless traders who visit SharePlanner.com have written me to ask about my journey from pushing paper and filling out forms as a contracts manager to trading full-time for myself. But, more important, they wanted to know what I did to become a successful part-time trader while holding a full-time job. That is, how was I able to trade while I was supposed to be working?

The Part-Time Trader

PART I

The Basics of Part-Time Trading

So How Much Do You Really Hate Your Job?

I had not always planned to become a full-time trader. Though I started trading at a young age, I always assumed I would just hold a normal job like everyone else. I did not know any full-time traders, nor did I have any friendships with those I would consider to be entrepreneurs.

I had a pretty good start to my career in writing contracts. Essentially, it required me to derive agreements between us and another entity that addressed all those boring terms and conditions, pricing, and the kind of product that we would be receiving. Sometimes I got to put on my Jerry Maguire hat and do a little negotiating of my own.

In other jobs, I had worked on Capitol Hill as an intern [insert derogatory joke here]. I graduated from an in-state college with high honors, but failed to land a job with my political science degree during an interview in the West Wing of the White House. That dot-com bubble started to burst, and with a pretty heavy recession under way, so it made sense to take any job that was willing to pay, even if the only thing I knew about contracts was the two-year commitment my phone carrier suckered me into.

■ Becoming Determined to Find a Way Out

I was on the fast track, and as one of my many bosses (yes, we had group leaders, managers, senior managers, program managers, and contract managers all hovering over us) put it, I was a "rising star" in the organization. In fact, less than a year into the job, I won the employee of the year award in this S&P 500 company for my "dedication" to teamwork after being part of a four-man team traveling to Indiana to help save a procurement system that had gone awry.

To be honest, I only signed up because they said I would get paid to eat three meals a day for the next two weeks on the company tab; fly on an airplane, which I had not done since I was 12; and get to stay in a hotel that had an indoor swimming pool.

The concept of the company picking up nearly everything during my time on the road was a foreign concept that later became known to me as *per diem*, (pronounced pər 'dēəm). So I got to go to Indiana during the heart of winter and call a bunch of people, explaining to them we did not mean to buy the "widgets" and "gadgets" our system accidentally ordered on our behalf. I went from being a contracts guy to crisis management. Throughout those long days, I managed to work my way through them because I would get my extra paycheck, requiring me to eat at the likes of McDonald's for breakfast, the Piggly Wiggly for lunch, and Ruby Tuesday's for dinner.

Then, to top it all off, I came back home to my southern dwellings as some sort of hero of our Indiana branch for essentially doing the same tasks that I would've done back home without getting paid extra to eat while doing it.

And that is how I became your corporate hero in year one, by being a stellar example of Teamwork Leadership in action.

Sure, the other candidate for the award happened to be some engineer that found a new way to split an atom, but yours truly stuffed his face with food at the local hog trough and happened to cancel a few bogus purchase orders in the process. As a result of all of this, I appeared to be some kind of "Team Player" to the powers that be.

Oh, yes, I guess it would help, too, that the vice president presiding over our organization was more interested in making his division look better than the rest, and yes, he was also a voting member (I later learned that conflicts of interest can be quite acceptable in the corporate world), and yes I got a crystal statue plus a $3,000 check! But that money was spent as fast as I could cash it because my guest at the award banquet happened to be a nice young blonde that I had been dating for a few years, and I had the itch to get a ring on her finger before somebody else did.

It was at that one and only moment of corporate greatness that I actually could see myself working for this company for maybe the rest of my career. Sad to say, that rising star I spoke of happened to sparkle just a little too soon.

Shorting My Own Career

From that time on I started a steady decline, not from a performance standard, because I actually did a good job at what I did, but more from a "this-job-sucks-and-there-has-to-be-something-that-is-better-to-do-with-my-life-than-this" perspective.

Let's just say it took me a while to figure what that was.

It Was Not in Real Estate

During the housing boom, a friend of mine, during one of our regular Monday lunches at a local spaghetti shop, proposed that we start building a house from the ground up and sell it for a HUGE profit. This close friend of mine, Nate Walker, said, "we will be swimming in cash," and to illustrate what he meant, he took an entire stack of napkins out of the dispenser at our table and tossed them up in the air.

I was sold on the idea.

The idea of buying and selling houses like everyone else was doing was music to my ears. Let's go find ourselves a plot of dirt and start building. His brother, Marcus, jumped right in with us, and we were off to the races. Luckily, Marcus was an engineer who could act as our general contractor. He pulled the permits; we got the house plan; we found people who would clear our land and another outfit that could install the septic and eventually contract having the walls and a roof installed. We did as much as we could on our own. To say the least, it was some major sweat equity we were putting into that house, with the belief that the napkins we had tossed in the air before would somehow morph into big-time cash and a new way of life for all three of us going forward. This was just the start.

It Started to Unravel

It did not quite go according to the way we planned it. Someone happened to get shot and killed down the street from where we were building. I learned there's nothing better than driving by a the chalk outline of a bloody dead man in someone's driveway as your realtor goes on to show you your future "dream home" just a few doors down.

We also had the neighbor's 13-year-old, who regularly shoveled his Rottweiler's poop onto our roof for his own kicks and giggles; pit bulls that managed to chase us to our cars on a regular basis; neighbors on the other side of us who painted their house hot pink; and a realtor who figured out some way to "adjust" his payout on the house for selling it without my knowing it.

We had bought the quarter acre of land for $56,000, and by the time we had finished building the house, we had two credit lines maxed out and almost $225,000 invested in the house. Had we only been able to short our own housing investment like I do with stocks, then that eventual sale price of $175,000 would've made for a great investment. Unfortunately, though, we were long and strong on a losing investment.

Stocks Would Be a Much Better Option for Me

One of the biggest turn-offs with real estate, besides the obvious monstrosity of a loss for me, was the liquidity difference between it and a stock. Fortunately, you can choose to invest only in liquid companies, and if the trade goes wrong, you can immediately get out of it for a loss. With real estate, you have to hold on to it; pay for upkeep, ungodly sums of taxes, and inspections; and guard against others making it even worse for you (like cold-blooded murder down the street).

We actually managed to keep costs under control, and if we were selling a house somehow without the land that we purchased to build it on, we might have been able to actually make a profit. Unfortunately, we had a piece of property that was worth about 1,000 percent more when we bought it than what it was appraised at when we sold it. That $56,000 land value was better valued at $5,000 a little over two years after we had bought it. Just to make things even better for us, we would later learn that the town that we chose to build our investment home in was one of the worst-hit foreclosure areas in the United States when that hyped-up real estate bubble finally did burst.

The only thing that gave me peace of mind is that in the misery of my real estate investment at the peak of the housing bubble, the losses were split three ways. I was quick to conclude, though, that I could cross real estate, homebuilding, and shoveling dog poop off of my list of career options to get me out of Corporate America.

Fortunately, during that same time, I had reignited my passion for stocks and trading in the financial markets.

I Loved Trading but Hated My Job—Something Had to Give

There are five classes of workers in Corporate America that I have come to learn. The first class represents those who embrace the politics of the workplace, the hierarchy, the rules, regulations, and processes that outline a job and the company at large. These individuals will typically bend over backwards to be noticed and to gain recognition, acceptance, and an additional title to their job description. Moreover, many of them will stab you in the back the first chance they get, and sometimes they will even spin you around, look you in the eye, and do the same to you from the front side, smiling while they turn the knife.

Corporate Hierarchy

In the long run, these people's aspirations and questionable tactics will often take them far in the company and find them on that enviable "fast-track" list to the top of the company.

Those at the Top Eventually, though, these same aspirations that served them well over the years will run them amok, as they will leave one too many bodies in their path, and that path will lead right to their own door-step. But those who can avoid this mishap will become chief executive officers, chief financial officers, presidents, and vice presidents. For the purposes of this book, I'll give the name "Edward" to this particular type of employee.

Those Who Wish They Were The second class comprises much of those same characteristics of the first class, but with one simple caveat: they have no chance at making it to the top, but they will spend an entire career trying to prove to themselves and to others that they can.

These types of people are brutal to be around. They are miserable and make those who have the unfortunate pleasure of working with them absolutely dejected. I had to work and try to get along with plenty of these types in my short corporate career. These are the types that have no problem throwing morals to the wind and ethics out the window when it comes to playing nice with coworkers. They will lie, cheat, and steal from you and everyone else.

I have a passionate distaste for these individuals because they represent the majority of those individuals that soured me on life in Corporate America and only flamed my desire to find a way out of it. Whatever you do, never trust these individuals, what they say, or what they tell you they are going to do because in all likelihood it is a facade of lies simply used to bait you into completing their agenda for self-gain.

These types of employees view their coworkers and those who work underneath them as their tools in a borderline sadistic kind of way. They are hell-bent on doing what satisfies them and realize a sense of accomplishment when they witness the misery of those for whom they are responsible. In fact, I would surmise that they probably get some kind of "rise" out of pushing people around and to the brink of seeing them lose it.

I would often try to make small talk with these individuals, believing that if I could get to know them on a personal level, that they would somehow take it easy on me, and not be such a royal head-case to work with. But I could not be more wrong.

Instead of forming some kind of camaraderie with the individual, they would turn on a dime if it suited their needs. And the most disturbing aspect of it is that they didn't seem to be troubled by it. Instead, they felt a sense of empowerment by it—like they knew you hated them, but they were content on simply flexing their muscles to demonstrate to you that they still wore the pants. For the purposes of this chapter and later ones, we will call this particular individual "Debbie."

As Harmless as the Swiss The third type of worker is probably as close as one can be to having the status of neutral. They are nonthreatening and try to do what is fair. They'll work an entire career, or close to it, for just one company. They are trusting and can be trusted. If they are your boss, life isn't bad. The problem is that they are hard to find. I had the rare opportunity to work for three of them. The drawback is that they can be pushed around some. While they are loyal, they will do whatever the person above them tells them to do. They thrive off of staying out of the limelight and controversy in general.

There was a time that I was able to show documented proof that a certain manager outside of my job function was lying about what I had done while working with him. When I laid out for my boss exactly how he had been lied to, he refused to act on it simply because the manager in question was friends with a vice president. Instead, I was awarded with a black mark on my record and the one likelihood that any promotion I was hoping for would be derailed by at least an additional three years, simply because intervening on my behalf would have required potential discomfort for the manager I served.

While I like working with these individual types, I don't expect much in the way of courage from them. They simply prefer going unnoticed so much that they, in moments of crisis, are unlikely to come through for you. But in the grand scheme of things, they will not interfere with your work unless absolutely necessary, and when they do intervene, it is usually at a much more nonthreatening level of reason. We'll call them "Gary."

The Malcontents Here's where we delve into the final two categories where one takes action and the other simply wishes he would. The latter hates his job. He's a pushover who needs the paycheck just like the rest of us, but the paranoia of losing that paycheck pushes him to do anything and everything asked of him by those above him and by his coworkers as well. The thought of not taking on every request made of him, and the requestor of those tasks possibly going to the boss man to complain, is all the motivation that he needs to essentially bow to anyone and everyone. They are the "Larrys" of the corporate world.

I have known plenty of these types, and, honestly, you have to pity them more than anything else. I have tried to talk to so many of them over the years, to embolden them to take pride in themselves and learn to use the magical word "no" when they are given excessive and unnecessary demands on the job.

Guilty as Charged I am guilty as well. I have, from time-to-time, taken advantage of their willingness to do anything they are asked to do and, in the process, dumping some of my own workload on them, simply because I knew they would not refuse to do it and that they would get the job done and usually done incredibly well. While they may be the ones that are most often stepped on, they are usually the most talented and overlooked employees in the organization.

I mean, why would I waste my time asking a Debbie or Edward when I knew that they would weasel their way out of helping me, all the while still finding a way to take credit for the task at the end of the day?

The skill set that the Larrys possess is there, and they should be thriving in their area of expertise. The only problem is that they are missing that critical element of faith that allows them to break away from the doldrums of a job they could not be more dissatisfied with, and venture out into their own and actually enjoy what they do for once.

Of all the people in the corporate world, this is the type you don't want to become. It results in long hours at the workplace, as well as anxiety, paranoia, and a sense of loss of one's own identity. I know this because I shared a lot of these characteristics, where early on in my career, I tried to be all things to all people. On one such occasion the boss man (actually boss woman at the time) came into my office about complaints about the backlog on my workload. I finally told her how I simply could not get all the work done at a pace faster than what it was coming in at; she was not mad or upset at all, but instead asked me why I never bothered to ask for help.

To me, it seemed like an admission of weakness on my part, but it really was not. At the end of the day, and not because of my own doing, I was able to offload my work, reduce my stress, and do better-quality work since the balance between reality and expectations finally evened out.

I truly would have been miserable; in fact, I would have probably had a breakdown had my superior not confronted me about it early on. Breaking away from the willingness to be another Larry and recognizing the need to not be everyone's "yes man" propelled me to eventually find a way out, which brings me to the last category: the "Ryan" employee.

An Inward Reflection

As previously mentioned, there is plenty of overlap between the Larrys and Ryans. They make great friends because of their mutual desire to leave the misery they find themselves in. In that sense, they have a lot in common and find each other to be a refuge for the frustrations they will not voice publicly. The ultimate difference between the two is that one will and one won't. Larry will complain and wish and dream of the day that he becomes self-sustaining and sufficient, while Ryan will ultimately do exactly that and brush aside the excuses that Larry makes for himself.

While the parallels between the aforementioned groups are obvious, they eventually pull away from each other. Larry will continue on the path that he has always been on, keeping his frustrations to himself, while Ryan will grow increasingly cynical in his job and hate it more and more every single day. While this person is dependent on his job and in need of it, he also realizes that steps must be taken in the present to begin the process of ultimately leaving his current career behind. This process, for me, lasted nearly four years. I had to start from scratch, but like any journey you take in life, no matter how long it is, it is paramount you make that first step.

Not an Easy Road to Take At times I wanted to give up. As a part-time trader, I experienced losing streaks and would grow tired and restless and would doubt my ability to ever be able to do it full-time. The winning streaks would allow for jubilation and a sense that freedom was right around the corner. I was a swing trader who was learning to trade around the balances of corporate life and managing a blog that would unknowingly become something entirely bigger one day.

My skills as a trader were solid; they had been honed over years of trial and error, through reading books that improved my mental state during the trade, and by others who—had I taken the advice they were spewing—would have derailed my entire operation. The biggest help to my trading was simply experience—that costly education that trading always requires, that we all wish to avoid, but in the end, are so glad we were able to experience.

Trading on the job has perks that full-time trading cannot provide, as it allows for the trader to polish his skills and experience trading's road traps without being adversely affected—assuming, of course, you are not relying on your paycheck to backfill your losses, instead of providing for life's essentials, you know, the important stuff like food, water, and shelter.

Embrace the idea that you are a part-time trader on track to become the real deal. Despite the sideshows I had allowed myself to become engaged in, with the hopes of finding a quick exit out of the corporate world (i.e., real estate), trading in the stock market was not just an exit strategy but a passion and love that was fully cultivated in my life. I did not see Apple as a company that made fancy phones and tablets but as "AAPL." Microsoft wasn't the creator of Windows and Xbox but simply a four-letter symbol: MSFT.

The journey at hand would not happen overnight, but I would get there with a plethora of success and mistakes, frustration, and excitement. I knew, though, that ultimately I'd get that yellow ticket to full-time traderhood while shedding the chains that had weighed me down in a job I immensely disliked.

Realize You Still Need Your Job

Life was so much simpler a hundred years ago. Of course, the opportunities for success were limited in comparison to what they are today, particularly with the creation of the Internet. Despite the lack of advancements, comparatively speaking, life was much more orderly. You knew your place in society. If you were born a Rockefeller, you knew that you were destined to leadership, innovation, and a life filled with luxury and surplus.

If you were born a "Joe Shmoe" like most of the population, you worked a 9-to-5 job. No weekend work and definitely nothing on Sundays. It might involve laboring with your hands on a Ford conveyor belt or working behind a desk counting beans. Either way, there were boundaries to life. You knew when you clocked out that you were done for the day. No e-mails, no pagers, no late night cell phone calls demanding that you come into the office because some shipment in Southeast Asia was delayed and wouldn't make delivery in Fresno, California, before 8 A.M.

Professional Paper Pushers

Perhaps I was made for a different era, but the times we live in now have drastically changed, and everything has become a bundle of complications. How often do you sit at a desk at work and your job skill may be a "quality engineer," but you are not really inspecting for quality but for how much a certain widget meets the requirements for a certain form. And in that form there are tons of questions, blanks, and check boxes that you are required to fill out for whether said widget passes inspection.

In reality, you aren't really a quality engineer but more like a professional "form-filler-outer." I know that might offend some, but it is true. Not noticing an inherent flaw in product when filling out these forms could result in the Occupational Safety and Health Administration (OSHA) or the Environmental Protection Agency (EPA) being in your office within 48 hours. The stress is real, and it affects us emotionally and physically. In my time working in Corporate America, three different individuals that I worked with committed suicide, with the reason often having its roots in their job.

Corporations have become so obsessed with process improvements, flowcharts, and metrics that they have made human ingenuity extinct and reasoning a lost art. The Garys, Larrys, and Ryans of the world feel helpless and relegated to being a chink in the armor of the Edwards and Debbies.

Getting back to how working in this day and age is so much more different than just a short time ago, I often consider e-mailing and the role that it plays in the workplace. I often recall how on any given day, I could get 150 to 200 e-mails and have Edward and Debbie coming by my office within an hour or two following up on that e-mail asking what the "status" was or better yet complaining why you had yet to reply to their e-mail. Of all the technological advancements we have seen, I think the worst one ever created was the blasted "cc:" option, where people who don't really need to be included in the e-mail are included anyway. That "cc:" is probably one of the most inefficient and unnecessary workplace concepts created to date, often leading to people being consumed with the task of how many people of importance they can include so that they can make their voice unnecessarily heard.

Too Many Cookies

On one such occasion, a person was trying to do a cookie fundraiser for their church, and somehow "cc'd" the e-mail out to over 15,000 employees when they only meant it for their department. The worst part of it all was that there was a 10-megabyte file included in the e-mail, and when it was sent out, people replied to all requesting that they be left off of the distribution list, and not knowing themselves they were replying to the entire organization. Most of the responses included that huge attachment that literally crippled the network for days with over 500 people replying nearly simultaneously to the large e-mail and attachment.

Who knew that an innocent e-mail coming from the hourly employees in accounts payable could be responsible for someone being fired for exposing the underlying weakness of "cc'ing" one too many people on a work e-mail? It literally had to be one of my top five favorite days on the job, because without a network, I could not do any work, and that meant I got to go home early and work from home—or I should say trade from home.

E-mail Paranoia

How about e-mail organization? I came across some of the most neurotic individuals in the workplace. They refused to ever delete a single e-mail, even one of those stupid spam e-mail forwards that they had received already a dozen times, the latest corporate staff reshuffle, or one of those newsletters offering the latest deals on Groupon. Seriously, people were that paranoid and uptight that the thought of deleting a single e-mail would eventually bite them in the butt should they ever need to access it and maybe result in their demise at the job they held.

If you are so paranoid about your job that you can't afford to delete a single e-mail, you really need psychological help. To add to it, these people, often the Debbies and Edwards, would have a category and subcategory for every e-mail type imaginable. Consider this: if the e-mail was about a past due invoice that the corporation had yet to pay, they would assign a special color for a certain priority level, then put it in the subcategory entitled "Company ABC" that followed the previous categories of "Accounts Payable," "Invoicing," "2012," "December." Yes, four subcategories deep.

Finding the Escape Hatch

Such categorization epitomizes workplace inefficiency, yet it calms the storms of paranoia for the Debbies and Edwards who feel the need to document every e-mail in such detail that if they actually tried to find the e-mail, they would spend more time trying to search out the actual folder the e-mail was deposited in than if they had simply left the e-mail in the original inbox.

Without getting too sidetracked on the pains of corporate life, it's worth reminding that while this book is about trading, it is also about recognizing the perplexities that exist among the common workers in Corporate America, and without the desire to break out from the stranglehold that it puts 99 percent of its employees in, they will be stuck just working for the boss man in hopes of one day finding a candle at the end of the dark tunnel. Unfortunately, what they find out is that the candle was never lit to begin with.

But with that said, you still need your job, and you need it in a bad way; otherwise, why would you still be working?

As you already well know by now, I hated my job and every aspect of it. There were times where I really felt like a prisoner in my own office. The reason was that biweekly paycheck that I was dependent on. My home, my cars, the food, and the health insurance were all possible because of this job, and that paycheck that took away my sense of identity as well as everything about my life that had seemed important to me.

Corporate Depression

Monday through Friday I dreaded. Saturday I enjoyed. Sunday, I became depressed, not because I was enjoying my second day off from the grinds of paper labor, but because I knew it was my last day off, and the moment I went to sleep that night, it would be only a moment before I woke up and realized a full five days of the "same-old, same-old" was ahead of me. It was a cycle that I dreaded and did not enjoy the least bit.

But in all of that, I found motivation—a motivation to leave what had become the norm of the past eight years and become the trader I knew I could become. I was a full-time trader in the making, and I was achieving that status as a part-time trader, whose success would eventually pave the way into realizing the career that for so long was only a distant fantasy.

As much as I would have liked for it to be something I obtained overnight, it wasn't. There were times when I would sneak out of the office and just drive. Drive anywhere. To the beach to reflect. To a random hotel where I would just roam the hallways as if I were actually staying the night there. I even at times would find the movie theater an escape into the realm of make-believe for two hours, and on Wednesday when they would even throw in a free bag of popcorn.

At times, I was depressed; at times, anxious and annoyed. The job paid the bills but emptied my sense of self-worth and value. When people asked me what I did for a living, I felt like a coward to tell them what I actually did, "Another piece of someone else's puzzle." A laborer, a Do-Boy, a willing slave on the plantation of Corporate America in which the chains were a paycheck I couldn't afford to rid myself of.

Extreme, yes, and ungrateful on my part for the opportunity to work and provide for my family? Absolutely! But my identity in life and who I felt God had created me to be were at conflict within. I couldn't reconcile the two with each other, and as a result, I lived my life day to day in discomfort and perplexed both intellectually and emotionally.

Despite all of that, I realized I needed my job. Otherwise, who would provide for my wife and child and their basic needs. As a result, I had to come to grips with the idea that quitting my job wasn't an option for now. I couldn't tell the boss man to "take this job and shove it." No, I needed it still, and despite my desire and growing skill set as a trader, I could not allow myself to compromise my job security and livelihood for my family and me. So I stuck with it. I grinded it out, and if it came down to a trade and getting an assignment done on time, I made sure the latter was taken care of first because if I allowed my trading to overtake the job at hand, I would never achieve the full-time trader status I so desperately desired. Instead, it would only result in my becoming a full-time failure.

CHAPTER 2

How Did I Become a Full-Time Trader?

Back when I was only 11 years old, an elderly Cuban lady, who was like a grandmother to me and the one who helped raise my mother, passed away. She left my three siblings and me $5,000 each for our college tuition. Since I was still about 7 years removed from going to college, it was important to find a home for this lump of cash until then. Thankfully, my father used it as an opportunity to teach me something that would pave the way for a lifetime of learning and, unbeknownst to him, start what would eventually become a livelihood for me.

We took that money and put it in the stock market. What a time to do it, too! It was the 1990s where everything went straight up. No pullbacks, no flash crashes, no quantitative casing. It was the stock market's gold rush, and everyone was clamoring to get in.

Desk jockeys were leaving their professions en masse to become self-employed day traders. If it was tech, then it must be had. If it was a "dot-com" stock, then sell the family farm for it. They rose from pennies per share all the way into the $100s. Anyone and everyone wanted in.

My Trading Foundation

My father took that money and guided me into choosing two mutual funds. One was an Alliance fund, and the other was a Putnam fund. We invested $2,500 in each one. After seeing my portfolio go from $5,000 up to $7,000, it became quite natural for me to grab the newspaper every morning, and instead of reading the sports section for the latest news on the Miami Dolphins, I flipped immediately to the business section and scanned for my funds in the midst of thousands of others for the latest price of that mutual fund. Over the next eight years, that small inheritance I had as an 11-year-old eventually was worth north of $30,000 by the time I graduated high school.

Beyond just the money that I was making during this time, I managed to keep a small notebook, and throughout different periods of my investment, I started plotting my own prices to see how each fund was rising in share price over time. I had no idea what technical analysis was at the time, but I was doing it in a pre-Internet age in the most rudimentary form known—by hand. It was not candles, moving averages, Bollinger bands, or any fancy form of price representation. It was price and price alone.

Rudimentary Understanding of Risk

What I learned during that time was that there was a wavelike feel to plotting the price of a stock. Even in the strongest of stocks, there was a $3 to $4 increase, then a $1 to $2 pullback, then another $3 to $4 increase, followed by that eventual $1 to $2 pullback. And the cycle would repeat itself. As my investment grew, I also saw where one of the two funds could take a momentary hit and really drag down the portfolio for a period of time despite the grand performance of the other fund I would be in. This is where I learned about risk. I realized that if I was in four or five funds and not putting all my money in just the two mutual funds I was currently in, then if one fund was lagging in performance, it would be much easier for the other four funds to pick up the slack and not allow for such a big performance hit to the portfolio. Now you could say I was becoming self-aware in regard to diversification.

Ultimately, the tech bubble would burst, just like the housing market later, and my investment of $30,000 shrank in a sudden and drastic manner. Luckily, before this happened, I bought myself my first computer for college (I was proud of my first 500-megabyte hard drive the computer came with), replaced the transmission in my car, and put a new set of tires on that clunker Oldsmobile I was driving. After all was said and done, my investment was worth only $10,000. While I might have walked away with over twice the amount I started with, I still had lost over $20,000 of potential profits that I could have done a better job of securing and not allowing the fantasy of sustained long-term growth to overtake my thinking. In the end, this became my lesson into the meaning of "portfolio capitulation."

A New Trading World

By this time I was in college, and while my understanding of the financial markets was better than most, during the next four years I became more interested in everything that college had to offer me rather than what was becoming of the new financial world with online brokerages and real-time quotes. At the end of the day, I had graduated from the University of Central Florida with my degree in political science, chose against going to law school, failed to land a job opportunity in the White House, found my future wife, and took a job at the first place I could find employment.

I remember the first online brokerage account I opened post college. I went with a discount brokerage that gave me a low commission rate only as long as I conducted my trades on Tuesdays. Strange, I know, but it was the cheapest outfit I could find, and I went with it. I ended up dumping a few hundred dollars a month on companies I found simply by staring at balance sheets, income statements, and cash flows and thereby eventually making a "sound" decision as to whether I should "buy" or move on to the next stock. I did okay, but it was more luck than any kind of special skill set I had working in my favor.

Turning against Invcsting

Early on, there was a defining moment for me that shaped my outlook on the time frame in which I chose to trade. I had put about $1,000 in a stock called Urologix (ULGX), shown in Figure 2.1. A penny stock at today's price, but when I bought it, it was trading at $8.00 per share. I bought myself a handful of shares, and ultimately I saw this price get as high as $16 per share. If you have followed my trading for any length of time, you know that is a gain I would book the profits on a hundred times over without even flinching.

But I was not the same type of trader back then. Not even close! I was a long-term investor. I was someone who had read all of Peter Lynch's

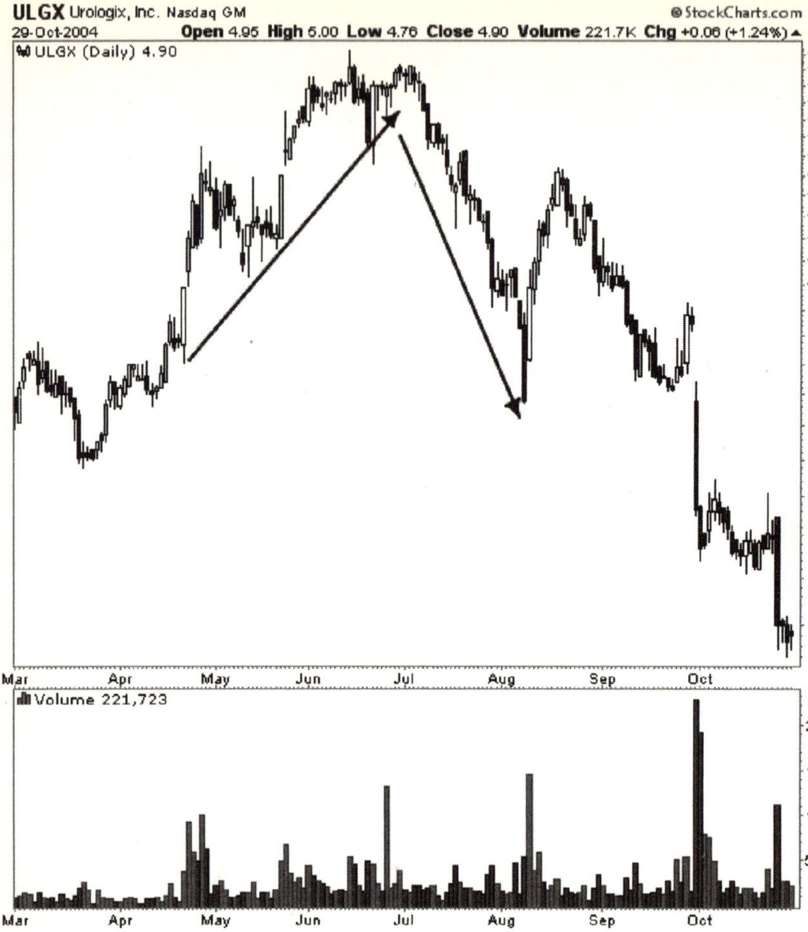

FIGURE 2.1 Urologix (ULGX)
Chart courtesy of StockCharts.com.

books and had learned to invest the Buffett Way. I even bought the Benjamin Graham and David Dodd book entitled *Security Analysis.* Of course, it was not to actually read it, but in hopes that the words would peel off of the pages and somehow enter into my brain (I still have the book sitting on my shelf today, with no intention of ever actually reading it).

With the limited understanding I had of the financial markets at the time, and the experience I was leaning on from the triple-digit growth from the 1990s that I had momentarily experienced, I was not going to be satisfied with just 100 percent in gains. I believed in the "long-term story" of this eventual sub-$1.00 stock. I married myself to its potential. So I rode this stock higher and higher, and eventually lower and lower, and below my eventual buy price, until I sold this stock later that year at a little more than $5 per share.

I was glad that this happened to me, though—honestly. Had I been successful in this trade, I might have bought into a flawed theory of long-term, "buy-and-hold" investing being relevant and a profitable strategy in the Internet age. I remember that day after ULGX had received the positive FDA news on a drug it was trying to get into production. A coworker in my office came in and I told him all about it. I tugged at my waistline and pulled at my imaginary suspenders as if I had made some genius investment move. He told me to sell and book those gains right away, but I was way above that whole short-term gains strategy. I was long term, baby! He begged me to sell it, having little financial background himself, but he showed me on the whiteboard in my office why I was foolish for not taking gains right then and there, but I ignored him completely.

Open-Minded to Becoming a Trader

It wasn't too long after that, in which I had a run-in at the local sandwich shop with my old friend Nathan. He told me how he had just made $400 in a single morning of trading from a stock pick off of his brother. I warned him that was dangerous business and that trading was just another form of legal gambling.

Deep inside, though, I was jealous. Every Monday, he'd tell about these stock picks his brother Matt was getting him into and how he was creating a great side income in the financial markets. As a long-term investor, $400 in a stock for me was probably worth a year of gains. Something was not adding up in my mind. I looked into it, and gave his brother Matt a call. We talked about trading, and he gave me a few stock picks to trade the next day. The first one was a $4 stock that I sold later in the day at $4.16 per share.

Wow! That felt dirty. I had just made 4 percent in a matter of hours on just one trade and I liked it. It didn't even feel right, almost like it was a crime to make a quick gain in a day's worth of work. For the next month or two, I would call him regularly, and Matt would give the latest picks he was trying to get into.

"Hey man, you got any picks today?" I'd ask.

"Sure, ABC if it pulls back to $10.25 and XYZ if it comes down to $7.40," he replied.

"That's over 20 percent away.

"Wait for it!"

Click.

I would do exactly what he told me to do and make a few bucks here and there, but then I realized here I was in my cubicle and I would be anxiously calling him asking: "Should I sell?," "Why is this stock dropping?," "Do I get in?," "What does a halt mean?" Relying on another person for stock advice just wasn't going to get me out of this job I clearly hated with a passion.

A lot of the stocks that I traded were downright "penny stocks." Some of these stocks traded at fractions of a penny. Essentially what I had done was create a formula with Matt where stocks that had risen 200 to 300 percent in a short period of time would eventually peak and pullback. What our formula sought to do was "catch the falling knife," which also happens to be a concept I am gravely against today in my own trading. Nonetheless, I was trading and the formula worked surprisingly well. I would later come to realize that it had a lot of the same characteristics of Fibonacci theory. The only problem with the formula came when the stock didn't perform like it should. I wasn't using stop losses, because my belief was to wait for the stock to come around to profitability. In two such instances it didn't, and boy, did it ever hamper the performance of my trading!

Road Bumps Ahead

MBA Holdings (MBAH) was my first disaster. I bought this stock at $0.015 per share. It had just made a massive run up to $0.08 and I thought I was buying it on the "cheap." There was a story behind this stock, and if it could pop just a few pennies, I would have made thousands on the trade.

It was exciting. Every day I had no idea if this stock would make my wildest fantasies come true or not. Instead, it taught me that I could have what I believed to be was an "iron-cast" formula for trading and beating the markets handily, but if I did not take the risk side of the trade as seriously as the profit side of it, I'd never make it in this business. Though I quickly learned this with MBAH, I did nothing to rectify this glaring problem in my trading style (much less my infatuation with stupid penny stocks). In fact, in my mind, the trade was not a red flag but an anomaly or unfortunate event that should be ignored.

Keeping Tabs in an Awkward Kind of Way There was one such occasion during the MBAH trade where I was on business travel at some event where our company was marketing our products to other companies. We were in Kansas City, Missouri, at the historic Union Station. I was away from my computer, smartphones didn't exist, and the travel laptop I was assigned did not do me much good outside of our hotel room. In order to keep track of my pathetic MBAH, I was relegated to taking regular breaks from the booth under the guise of taking an "important phone call," needing to buy something to drink, or having to use the restroom.

I found this little room tucked away near the bathrooms, where it was unlikely that anyone I knew would find me. My broker at that time was TDAmeritrade. I took out my flip phone, dialed the 800 number that allowed me to get a quick quote of any stock in the market. But I had to say each letter of the stock symbol into the phone mouthpiece.

Let me just say—for those who ever walked by me while I was doing this, it would usually turn heads for those in proximity to my voice. Roughly 80 percent of my attempts to get a stock quote would end in "Sorry, I did not understand, please try again." And if the stock symbol contained a "B," "D," "P," "V," "E," "N," or "T," you could rest assured the phone conversation would be difficult one to get any stock quote for. Trying to get a quote for MBAH sounded something like this:

"Welcome to TDAmeritrade's automated phone service. You can either say the company name or symbol."

"M . . . B . . . A . . . H . . .," I would state punctually.

"I'm sorry, I did not understand, please state the company or stock symbol again." It replied.

"Eeemmmm . . . beeeee . . . A . . . aechhhhh," I said, more clearly than before.

"MDAS—Med Assests, Incorporated" and it would proceed with the stock quote for the particular company.

Then I would actually start getting personal with the automated quote service.

"No! I said M . . . B . . . A . . . H, you piece of trash," in my lame attempt to hurt the feelings of the voice recording.

"NOK—Nokia Corporation," it retorted.

Literally, this would continue for the next five minutes or so until I got a stock quote and my focus would become how many fractions of a penny had the stock gone up or down by since the last successful quote attempt. On this particular occasion, my stock was up, not overall—just on the day. That made me feel like a successful trader for the current day at hand, and I proceeded back to the booth after a 15-minute absence.

I would repeat this cycle 10 to 15 more times throughout the convention because my mind could focus only on what MBAH might be doing. The process of dialing the phone number was exhilarating. What if it rallied a half penny's worth since the last time I had phoned in?

More times than not, I would be disappointed. I was essentially immersed in a legal gambling habit known as "penny-stocking." While I thought I might have some great skill set in finding the right penny stocks to trade, all it took was one broken link in the chain, and the strategy went to trash on me, and weeks of gains vanished in the blink of an eye.

Leaving Penny Stocks Behind

After moving beyond the penny stocks, I quickly began formulating ways to manage my risk better. It simply wasn't enough to find a decent stock pick. I needed to be able to manage risk on the stocks that failed. This was the point where I had come to grips with my own fallibility as a stock picker.

I would never get them all right, and sometimes I would not even get the majority of my stock picks right. If I was to become a successful part-time trader and eventual full-time trader, then I needed to pay more attention to mitigating risk than worrying about the possible profits that could be made (sometimes those profits were a mere fantasy not embedded in reality).

Let's face it, profit opportunities will ultimately come. Even if it is through pure randomness, if you trade stocks, you are going to have some winning stocks, no matter how green or new you are to the practice. Once I came to realize that trading stocks is much more about the skill of handling losses than some rare ability to cash in on outsized gains, or being some "genius stock picker," I was able to take a positive step forward in becoming a better trader with the ultimate goal of detaching myself from the rigors of the corporate world.

In Search of a Shortcut But it wasn't full steam ahead from there. I would subscribe to various newsletters, from sub-$10 trades that borderline killed my account when the stocks would report earnings, to a newsletter that claimed to have the greatest stock picks, the latter of which would provide four or five trades per day, and would report to you only the highest price the stock hit that day, not the price at which he actually sold the stock. Essentially, he was helping me with only 10 percent of the trade, and as long as it went $0.01 over the entry price at some point, he would dock the stock a winner.

When I subscribed to these newsletters, I would literally get to work and have to start putting in my alerts for the day based on the entries that were posted. One way to create havoc in your work and trading balance is to introduce day trading to it. Unless your job involves sitting at your desk and doing next to nothing, then you should go ahead and rule out day trading as your preferred trading strategy. These stocks that the newsletter would put out were often in the $3 to $5 range. He would give the picks, and it was my job to figure out when to get out of them. To think I could actually get work done was a pipe dream. I would have to work through lunch and stay a while afterwards just to make sure I put in an honest day's work.

Once the market opened at 9:30 A.M., you can bet I was glued to my quote feed and streaming charts to see the action and which stocks I was jumping into. The worst was when someone would schedule a meeting in the morning and basically thwart any ability to successfully manage those trades. But don't underestimate my own foolishness—I'd still put my orders in and pray to God that any orders that were filled would somehow be profitable by the time I came back into the office. To put it mildly, those stock picks weren't so great and represented an attempt at a shortcut in my learning curve at ultimately becoming a full-time trader.

False Hopes in Books Other problems existed where I would get so pumped up about a myriad of books that I would read, that upon completing them, I would try to mimic their trading system or strategy and instead of duplicating their successes, I would simply further delay my own development. I found myself trading options, futures, exchange-traded funds (ETFs), and stocks. I had experimented with literally every kind of trading vehicle while working full-time.

Ultimately, I would get nestled into a trading groove that would not seek to hit home runs every time at bat, but instead I would look to make steady and consistent gains over the course of a myriad of trades. My obsession was no longer with finding great stock picks but finding excellent risk opportunities.

I did not want to diddle-daddle in a stock in hopes that it would eventually work out. Instead, I wanted trade setups that offered a quick way of knowing whether the stock would go in my favor or not. If the stock worked out, I'd stay in. If not, the stop loss I set made it to where I would quickly realize whether the trade would work to my benefit or not. Therefore, I wasn't going to hang around for long as my stops would do the work, if the trade moved against me.

My Experience with Trading at Work

One thing is certain—I have literally traded in every office environment humanly possible. I have worked in my own personal office, which is obviously ideal; I have shared an office (not ideal); I have been in a cubicle; and even shared a cubicle. Heck, there was one time where my desk was located in in the middle of a common area, surrounded by seven offices staring directly at my computer screens. More challenging aspects of trading occurred when I was traveling in excess of 25 percent of the time. But nonetheless, it is possible to do so.

There was one particular time where I actually came back from a conference an hour away, and the next day at work, I could not even find where my office was. The brilliant manager thought it could not wait one more day and decided to move my office down the hall to be paired up with someone else. Exhibiting her lazy managerial skills, she actually managed to throw away a number of important documents, none of which was more personal to me than my college diploma that was lying on my desk because I had been waiting for the special-ordered frame to arrive in the mail. Her reasoning for doing so was since everyone had already gone home for the day, she did not want to haul everything down the hall to my new stomping grounds.

Accepting the Cards I Was Dealt

Trading at work no doubt added a heap of stress to my life. I knew that if I did not figure out how to do it, I would never have a way out of this job that was sapping the very life out of me. Since the stock market trades only from 9:30 A.M. to 4 P.M. Eastern, I really didn't have a choice but to figure out how to balance the two.

Now if you go into your boss's office and say, "Hey, boss man (or boss woman, as was often the case), I just wanted to run by you the idea of my trading throughout the day while on the job. I'm going to get all my work done, but a lot of my time will be spent staring at my computer screen watching stock prices," I am pretty sure your boss is going to puke all over your idea. In fact, you will likely add yourself to the fast-track demotion list. That is because perception is reality to the boss.

You tell him you are trading, and he is going to assume you are not a "company man." You are not supposed to have career aspirations outside of your job. Outside aspiration is not something that corporations like to compete with. The dirty little secret that corporations never like to admit is that 80 percent of their workers hate working for them. They do it out of need, not desire.

I have met people who will tattoo their favorite football team on their back, despite their performing in the cellar of their league. There was even an individual who tattooed the Mitt Romney campaign logo despite Romney's losing in the 2012 election. But tell me one person that has ever tattooed the logo of the company for which they work on any part of their body.

The point is that most people look forward to Fridays, holidays, and retirement, not Mondays or the end of vacations. Corporations as a whole put forth the image to their employees that there is no greater experience than working for them with unbridled loyalty. So don't go parading to the boss man that you have interests outside of work, or drawing up the plans that will allow you to live independent of anything they can offer. If someone told me just that, it would be music to my ears. To them, it is treason.

Flying Undected

I learned that I would have to trade below the radar because the moment that my trading became known would also be the moment that my trading plan came apart. I walked on pins and needles. If someone asked me about the stock market, I would give them a response that was equal to "What's that?" And trust me, that wasn't easy to say.

I loved talking about stocks. When the market was tanking over 300 points on the Dow and folks around me were freaking out about it, I wanted to stand atop my desk and let them all know that I was making money while they were all losing it. I wanted to give them all a 101 lesson on what shorting a stock meant and why they should have been doing it at the same time I was.

Instead, I simply shared in their agony and agreed with them that it was probably the fault of day traders or state some other popular generalization, such as "I guess it's time to get out!" I did this for years on end, up until I gave them my two-week notice. Then everyone just assumed that I was going to learn how to trade stocks, unaware that I had been doing it since I was just 11 years old in various shapes and forms.

There were a couple of people through it all that I did ultimately trust, but I was limited in what I told even those individuals. One person who was closing in on retirement did not really need his job any longer and was a short-timer with one foot already out the door. I'd go by his office all the time and talk about the trades I had on, as did he, and what he was thinking in regard to market direction and areas of improvement in my own trading. I always picked up interesting tidbits on trading, as he had practically seen it all—some of which I still hold very dear to this very day.

One particular tip he brought my attention to was the amount of trading that took place on the first trading day each month. Often, this day brings huge price swings in excess of 1 percent in the major indices due to the huge influx of funds receiving new money and trying to position themselves accordingly with the fresh capital injection they received.

What is even more interesting is that the first day of the month is often streaky, meaning it is often easy to decipher what will occur based on what took place over the past four to five months of price action on those first-of-the-month trading days that preceded the current one. In particular, when there is a strong uptrend intact, almost every month will result in large gaps up on that first day of the trading month, as shown in Figure 2.2.

FIGURE 2.2 Gaps On the First Day of the Trading Month
Chart courtesy of StockCharts.com.

Don't Obsess Over Profits

One of the traits you do not want to possess when trying to advance your part-time trading career is to take on more than you can do. Early on, I figured if I could trade bigger and be successful at doing so, I could shave some years off of my career in the corporate world. This was a big mistake. Early on, I was trading only one or two positions. I had a basic understanding of technical analysis, but I had not gotten to the point where I would "count the cost" before I entered a trade, meaning I did not weigh the risk of losing or being stopped out of a particular trade setup, as well as being stopped out of that position and simultaneously being stopped out of all my other positions as well, which can happen from time to time.

More Money Than I Could Afford to Lose

On one particular occasion early on in my trading career, I was trading with only a few thousand dollars. I had been on an incredible win streak, and like most newbies to the craft, I assumed that I could keep that going on indefinitely, because somehow, in my mind I had convinced myself that I had "arrived."

Rather than be wise with my capital, I thought it would be more prudent to increase the amount I was trading with. So I took the capital I was currently trading with and found the means to double it from some of the money in my savings account. I was excited! I had a whole new world of trading before me—more positions I could apply my stellar technical analysis to and more positions I would profit from. Taking a loss never entered my mind. Instead of trading two or three stocks, I took on seven new positions, which up to that point was something I had never done before.

That same day I had found the seven stocks that I wanted to buy. Yes, I could not wait for the right trades to come to me; instead, I had to find seven stocks that I could buy the following morning, regardless of overall conditions. I had the money, and I was going to use it.

Throughout that morning, I added those desired positions to the portfolio one by one. I even put on stop losses that made sense and managed risk appropriately. I went to sleep that night, not thinking a single bit about what I had done. I was confident, excited, and in my mind made a bold move that one day I will look back on as being "genius." This was my moment—the kind of stuff that would be written about in a book one day (that I was right about!).

I woke up the next morning, the futures were up, and everything looked good. I had my stop losses in because that was the best way for me to manage risk. The opening bell at 9:30 A.M. could not come soon enough. When the profit/loss total was flashing green in the early going, I was ready to start projecting my course into the future already (hindsight I should have been selling, not projecting). Maybe seven positions isn't enough, I probably need more capital, perhaps enough to trade 10 to 15 simultaneously.

Margin was never something I considered using, but perhaps I should reconsider. I had a meeting that day coming up, and, as I'll reiterate throughout this book, you have to attend to the responsibilities of your job and make sure it remains the first priority or no matter how good a trader you are, if you don't have enough to trade full-time, you must take your job seriously.

A Fresh Dose of Market Reality

I went to the meeting; it was a short department meeting that lasted all of 30 minutes. Once it was over, I hurried back to the office. I was excited about what I thought I would see. The walk down the hallway seemed to take forever, but once I got behind my monitor at the desk, logged in, and popped open the command center I was trading off of, I saw nothing but red!

The S&P gave up what was otherwise a great day, and was now trading—2.2 percent in the red. Those positions that I had gone into the day prior were getting slammed. Apparently, Alan Greenspan had flapped his lips, and the market did not embrace his comments.

My stop losses were roughly 7 to 8 percent away from the entry price, and they were flashing some major red. I honestly could not believe my eyes. How could this have happened? I felt cheated. Violated. Taken advantage of. Heck, I wanted a dadgum refund! Nonetheless, there are no do-overs in the market.

With one eye opened and the other eye closed, I squeamishly looked at the profit/loss on the day. It was more than what I had ever experienced in my lifetime for a single day. I had never lost even $1,000 in a day, much less $2,000. But that was how much I was down, and my stop losses were not even close to being hit. The thought of getting taken out at my original stop losses was too much to bear. The market looked like it had gone off of some cliff with no bottom in sight.

I really didn't know what I should do. Continue losing the money that I really shouldn't have been trading with in the first place and show a "trader's discipline" of following my plan, or panic, sell now, and cut my losses while I could.

I chose the latter and did a fire sale on all my positions as fast as I could. I was emotional, as furious as one could be, and I proceeded to raise my mouse into the air and slam it down as hard as I could on my desk, not once, not twice, but six times! The bottom part of it cracked into multiple pieces and was rendered useless. To make matters worse, one of the stocks that I thought I had sold out of did not go through as I had inputted the order incorrectly. I watched that stock drop further with no way to stop it because my stupid mouse was broken, and I did not know the necessary shortcuts offhand on my keyboard to close out the order I was so desperate to close.

But before I could even leave for the folks upstairs in the information technology (IT) department, two ladies hurriedly came inside my office wondering what in the name of Sam Hill that noise was. Thinking quick on my feet, I made up some lame excuse about how I dropped the mouse by accident, which somehow or another created a thunderous noise that probably managed to shake the cubicles outside of my office. I doubt they were convinced of my story, but it was not my priority to convince them otherwise right now. I had a position still that was bleeding through the nose, and I had to get upstairs to the IT group and swap out my mouse for one that actually worked. After another lame excuse for why my mouse was in three separate pieces and the exchange for a new pointer, I finally made my way back downstairs, past the ladies now gossiping about what really happened, and then got out of that last position.

A Learning Experience, Indeed

Needless to say, there were two major lessons to take away from this episode of bad judgment that I exhibited early on in my trading career. First, I had placed the stop loss that might have made sense technically, but psychologically they were an absolute disaster and would eventually be exposed as such. I placed my stops 7 to 8 percent away from my entry price. This might have been acceptable for me when I traded with less money and fewer positions, but I took on an amount of capital that even from the onset I was uncomfortable with, and did not even know it. Take an average stop loss of 7 percent across seven positions and I'm looking at the potential of a combined 49 percent in losses—not against the portfolio, thankfully, but against my average position size, which is still a ton to lose.

Understanding Risk Aversion

I am risk averse. I don't like the threat of losing a lot of money in my trading. When I do, I become irrational in my thinking. Therefore, I keep my losses on a percentage basis relatively small. Today, I trade with 2 to 4 percent average stop losses. If the stop loss has to fall outside of this number, then I'm not going to take it, no matter how promising the setup is to the upside.

Back then, I never counted the cost if all seven positions went against me. Even had half of the positions gone against me while the rest remained at breakeven, I probably would've still conducted a similar type of fire sale—with probably the same amount of emotion, too. I was not trading within my tolerance for risk, and as a result, I made a decision that was irrational.

You can guarantee yourself that when you trade outside of your tolerance for risk you will undoubtedly make the wrong decision regarding your trades and capital allotted to you. That is exactly what I did, and as a result I had to pay for it dearly. Had I let my original stop losses play out, I would have been profitable on five of the seven trades that I took losses on prematurely. Because my emotions were out of check, and I was trading beyond what I could tolerate from a risk standpoint, I completely mismanaged the trade. The original trades that were made were fine, but the trader clearly was not.

A Simple Step for Controlling the Emotions

This brings me to my last point. Do not watch the profit/loss total for a day or for a given position. Trading is not about dollars and cents; it's about price and volume. Know beforehand how much you are willing to risk on a single trade and across multiple trades at once. After you determine that, there is no reason to follow the profit or loss you are incurring on a given trade. It will only stir up the emotions. Furthermore, don't look at your profit or loss until after the trade is completed. For some out there, you may want to see if you can go an entire month without looking at the bottom line.

Profits (or losses) are tied to your position size and how much you are risking. You can determine all of that before you ever enter the trade. But it has nothing to do with the stock you are trading and the subsequent price action thereafter. If you watch the dollars and cents, you will start to do what I am very susceptible to doing. If I'm up a few thousand on a trade, I will begin thinking of what I can buy with that money, or how I can add that money to my son's college tuition or some other materialistic motive. But what is it good for? What does that have to do with trading in the least bit? Absolutely nothing!

Decisions on buying or selling have to be based on price and volume and any overlays, indicators, or oscillators that you might choose to use. Basing it on a dollar sum is foolish business and will only cause you to trade based on your emotions. Trade what the charts are telling you. If the trend is up, and there is solid support underneath it, then trade accordingly. If you are up 10 percent on a trade and want to ensure that a winning trade does not turn into a losing trade, then tighten the stop loss in an appropriate manner. But do not look at the profits that you might be making and say, "$500 is a lot of money. I'm taking my profits now and my wife, kids, and I are going to the Sizzler."

The percentage gained or lost on a given trade is much easier to manage from a mental standpoint than are the dollars made or conceded. Seeing it with your own eyes brings a sense of realism to the trade that allows you to identify with the trade on very personal terms. Do not allow that to happen. Many platforms, like ThinkorSwim, for instance, allow you to block the actual portfolio value as well as the gains/losses feature on a given trade. I am not saying that you should be oblivious to the destruction you might be causing to your portfolio, because that can be seen by simply looking at the past performance from a percentage standpoint. Avoiding the actual dollars you are making or losing on a given trade will help you to eliminate a great deal of the emotions from the trade that could lead you to making a fire sale–like decision similar to the one I engaged in early on.

Emotions are killers in a trade, and if you allow that to creep into your workplace and its responsibilities, then you are creating double trouble for yourself, as you will become inept not only in your trading but likely in your job as well. An influx of emotions from trading often paralyzes the trader, and if that happens, you are not likely to be fit for your real job either.

Where Wall Street Meets the Office

I've always been a big fan of the NBC show *The Office*. Besides the fact that the show itself is absolutely hysterical, I was always able to identify with the character Jim Halpert. Here was an individual that was probably the best employee in his office, yet completely unable to relate to his job function or actually find any passion for what he did each day. It is no wonder that by season nine of the show, Jim is trying to find his own escape from the Dunder Mifflin branch in Scranton, Pennsylvania, to a new start-up company that identifies more with who he is as a person.

How can one possibly be passionate about selling paper? That is how I felt about where I was in my career. As a contracts manager, I would simply fill out countless forms each and every day. Every once in a while I would be allowed to negotiate a multimillion-dollar contract, but before I could get excited about that, I would be faced with having to follow a stack of processes so detailed that it practically covered the way I was to regulate my breathing while I was at the negotiation table. Despite the impressive dinner talk that "negotiating multimillion-dollar contracts" was, the reality of actually doing it was very robotic and restrictive. There was no opportunity for me to be like Jerry Maguire.

To say the least, I was inundated with about as much paperwork to fill out as Jim Halpert was in selling it—form after form, process after process, metric after metric, and report after report. I became miserable in my job. I was a person who needed to use the brain cells that God had given me, yet in order to do that there would have been a clearly outlined process determining how I could use them, too. I was allowed only to follow processes and nothing more.

■ Work Ambivalence

Furthermore, there became this obsession with reports. I was considered a salaried person, but there was literally a requirement that stated we had to account for every bit of our time on the job down to one-sixth of an hour. There were these things called project codes, where every assignment we were given had a six-digit number assigned to it. Project codes were like currency. If you had project codes, you had work. If you did not have a project code, it meant you did not have any work to do, and ultimately it meant you would probably be shown the exit door.

I never had an issue with acquiring project codes because I did good work on the job and, frankly, I was a noncontroversial person. If the boss man wanted me to do something, I did it. I really did not care if what they wanted me to do made sense, nor did I care if the assignment I was asked to do was strategic and in the company's interests. There were plenty of people who wanted to be the Donald Trump of the workplace and thought that they were shrewd and genius in their business activities. Maybe I could have been more like that as well, but I did not try to be. I was not worried about seeing the business succeed because like good Jim Halpert, I was not involved enough in its success or failure. I just did my job and did what was necessary to keep getting paid.

Nonsensical Reports

We also had to fill out biweekly activity reports. Sounds exciting, right? But there were so many other reports from financial projections, contract metrics, supplier report cards, work-flow expectations, and program report cards that when I actually got around to doing the activity report that was to detail what I had actually done, I would typically list 40 percent of my time being spent on reporting on what I was doing. That's right—we were so consumed by metrics and reports that I spent roughly 40 percent of my time having to detail what I did with the remaining 60 percent of the time on the job. That is the definition of *circular logic*—reporting on what you are reporting on.

I honestly do not think they cared what I put in those reports; they just wanted them so they could, through some way of metamorphosis, know what was going on because they required that we fill out these reports, not that they actually planned on reading them. From time to time, I would drop a ludicrous comment in the activity report. Under the section entitled "Ways to Improve My Workplace Efficiency," I would write, "Fill out fewer of these pointless reports."

Pretty brazen, I know, but honestly, this B-level employee with a personal identification number of 239405 was unlikely to be highly thought of enough to actually read one of the 104 reports that I submitted each year, in conjunction with the other 30 employees in the department, which meant that in the course of one year our department expected its employees to fill out a combined 3,120 activity reports. Great use of time, wouldn't you say?

The point of this is, even if you find the strains of business pointless, you have to do them. It is perfectly acceptable to hate them, even complain to the non-powers-that-be about them, but do not neglect them. One of the most important aspects of trading in the workplace is not becoming a drag on the organization and a resultant problematic employee by placing a greater priority on the actual trading itself than the work you are required to do to stay employed.

Workplace Scalawag

Many times the events that took place in the workplace puzzled me. There was a guy named Joe, a clown and wannabe "Edward" who, despite his insignificance to nearly everyone who worked with him, tried to place himself on a pedestal above his coworkers and equal with every executive and director he fell underneath in hopes that someone might take him seriously.

One day, while working on Christmas Eve, he insisted that I process an invoice that I was not supposed to submit and have accounts payable cut a check that same day, which actually takes about a week, for reasons unbeknownst to me. And he wanted me to overnight that check to a supplier so that it would arrive the next day, on Christmas, which was also impossible since that was a federal holiday and the post office doesn't even deliver on that day.

This was all because that date was the cutoff for our monthly revenue forecasts. Since he was short on his financial forecasts that month, he insisted on this payment being made. He was so adamant that he tried to give me the Lyndon Johnson treatment and slam his fist down on my desk and demand that I "do it or else" and then proceeded to walk out of my office. My first instinct was to look for the nearest camera (as if that existed) and give it the Jim Halpert shoulder shrug, with the confused eyebrow raise and bottom lip grimace.

My next thought was to knock this punk's lights out, but I withheld—not because I couldn't get the job done but because keeping the status quo was more important for me. I had a nice office at the time (with a rare window view, too, though the actual window was outside in the hallway) where I could do my trading without any significant interference.

Now, had I reported him to Human Resources or the boss man, it might have been determined that they needed to move my office somewhere else so that I did not feel threatened by the dude with the funky mullet haircut and "I'm a tough guy" goatee. If that happened, who knows where I would wind up?

Offices were at a premium in that building, and I didn't want to lose the one I had, especially one with a quasi–window view. I was able to trade unfettered in my current location, my performance was solid, and I wanted it to stay that way. So Joe got his way. I submitted the invoice for processing, not because I was worried about him and what he might do, but because keeping the status quo and being viewed as a team player was more important than stroking my own ego as the office Don Quixote. But I am pretty sure the check didn't arrive on Christmas Day as he had hoped for.

If you work long enough, you'll find that there are challenges like this in different shapes and sizes that will affect your ability to trade successfully in the workplace. Your response is critical, and to stay cool at all times will help to ensure that you do not draw unnecessary attention to yourself. The last thing you want is to be micromanaged.

■ Decide How Successful You Want to Be at Your Job

It did not take long before I realized that I could not be successful in my job if I was going to be successful in my trading. I wanted out, but for me to get out, I would have to find that balance in the meantime of being a "good company man" while making sure my trading did not get sidetracked, but steadily increase my portfolio value all at the same time. I knew that rising up the company ladder, or getting on that "promotional fast-track" list would not happen if I was going to take my trading to the next level. A Bible verse that I learned as a child stated, "No one can serve two masters, for either he will hate the one and love the other, or he will be devoted to the one and despise the other" (Matthew 6:24).

Just as it was true in how we worshipped God, it was also true in my work. I could not pursue two careers simultaneously. Either I was to excel in my job as a contracts manager, which I was fully capable of doing (but did not want to do), or I would excel in my trading. For obvious reasons I chose the latter.

The Boss Man Reviews

With that, I had to guard my expectations. Each year we had to be reviewed in our current job position. Now, let me tell you something—this was a total circus. Later in this chapter I will discuss how the organization had pitted all of its employees against one another and how they would create only a certain number of possible promotions, each year, and purposely below the usual amount that would be deserved. But to make it worse, during our reviews, they would make my peers review my performance from the past year. That's right—I would get to choose five people who would critically review my performance. It was literally a corporate "Hunger Games" scenario.

Creating a Friendly Coalition This was often a problem for me because, frankly, some of those around me knew I did not go the extra mile in my job and that I was indifferent toward aspiring for more responsibility. But, with that said, I did do a good job at what I was asked to do. That, however, did not help much when they would ask such questions as:

- Does employee exhibit a team-like attitude?
- Does employee take the necessary steps to achieve "next-level resolutions"?
- In daily activities does employee exhibit a mindset toward company shareholders?
- Do customers experience increased levels of satisfaction when interacting with employee?
- As a corporate citizen, does employee maintain mutually beneficial relationships with suppliers and coworkers?

As you might imagine, on the surface I probably would not fare too well on the peer reviews when they came around each year. But I was smart about how I approached it. My approach to peer reviews was similar to the CBS show *Survivor,* as I would try to create alliances with various employees, since I was having a secret affair with the stock market and wanted to guard my clandestine operation from being exposed. If I were going to successfully do that, you better believe I would have to create some alliances for myself.

The Approach Now I couldn't just go up to another employee and say, "Hey, if you give me a good review, I'll give you a good review." It just does not work that way (unfortunately). That kind of strategy will (1) make you sound incredibly desperate and likely get turned down like a sixth-grader at an eighth-grade dance; (2) get you a horrendous review that will create the opposite effect of what you were hoping to achieve (in fact, they may snitch on the request in your review itself), or (3) possibly land you in the boss man's office for, let's just say, soliciting a positive review, which in the boss man's eyes will make you a "bad corporate citizen."

That means you must be doing pretty crummy work (whether you actually are or not), so much so that you are going around trying to convince others to provide you with a good review. Congratulations—you are now on the boss man's radar.

The Good Samaritan

Here's how you do it. For however many employees you need to review you, find those who are the least vocal and controversial in your department. Stay away from the loudmouth brown-nosers—they will throw you under the bus faster than you can imagine, no matter how friendly you think you guys are with each other.

Once you have identified these individuals, go to their offices, one by one. Strike up a friendly conversation about something you both have a mutual interest in or something you will both be able to agree on. Stay away from controversial topics, and at the end of it, try to migrate it into the drudgery of self-reviews and how time consuming and useless they are. As working members of the proletariat, you'll likely be able to agree on this.

After you have finished yapping, go ahead and close out the conversation by saying something to the effect of "Looks like I better get back to my cubicle before someone notices" and nonchalantly exit the office, but right before you are out of arm's reach of the office door, spin around, grab the door frame with one hand, and say, "Oh, and on the topic of employee reviews, if you need an extra peer review, send me a request, and I'll make sure to hook you up." Then smile and proceed back to your desk (for real this time).

Once you have done this, you'll soon get a request from this person because no matter how great an employee he or she is, there is nothing that a person likes more than assurance in an insecure work environment. I would say this strategy worked well for me nearly every time, and 9 times out of 10, I would have a peer review request from that person by day's end.

Peer Kindness Now that you have received that request, don't sit on it. Oh, no—fill it out right away. If they ask for any negatives on the person, simply write "N/A" or "Employee excels in this area." The boss will be happy to see that someone else views them in such high regard. But when you send it to your boss, also blind copy (the dreaded "bcc:" field on an e-mail) the individual the review so they can read the high regards that you hold them in. They will be forever grateful to you for it. They will never tell on you for doing this because they will be so thankful for the kind words you said and are vulnerable enough to believe that it will somehow help advance their own careers.

They will be elated with the kind words and wonder what their boss is thinking when he reads it. Remember, it is key that you blind copy them on the e-mail because when they see with their own eyes what you actually wrote, they will be primed and ready for you take the next step.

Reaping What You Sow Once you have your coworker's peer review out of the way, you then proceed to send them a review request for yourself. Unless they are some kind of ruthless barbarian (and you would know it if they were), they will gladly accept this, as they are still riding on cloud nine from what you said about them, and will write a glowing review about you as well.

Maybe it won't be as over the top as the one you did for them, but they definitely are not going to throw you under the bus. And out of a need for reciprocity and "corporate citizenship," they are likely to blind copy you on the review they send to your boss as well. It is that whole "You scratch my back, I'll scratch yours" mentality."

Filling Out Your Own Review

Seven years after having won the employee-of-the-year award, I was still finding ways to incorporate the fact that I got the award in nearly every one of my yearly reviews. When it came to the section entitled "Accomplishments,"

I always would refer to that one glorious day in my corporate career that, for a moment in time, made me think I was one of them—no, no, better than the rest of them, as if I could dominate the industry and become some kind of tycoon in the process. Unfortunately, that feeling lasted for only about 48 hours. After the curtains had dropped and the pageantry subsided, I realized I was left with just a useless crystal paperweight that measured about 1/35 the size of the Eiffel Tower.

Even more telling was the fact that when I came into work the following Monday, I thought somehow I would receive a hero's parade of some kind. Not a chance. Most were disgruntled that I had won such an award and had done so less than a year into the job—for good reasons, too, though it might have felt good at the time. There is no doubt that the award itself was nice, and so was the bonus I received, but it was all pointless in its ultimate meaning and the false sense of hope that it could give someone.

Not for employee year-end reviews, though. And had I stayed there for 25 more years, I would have probably still been using that one solitary award as part of my yearly review.

Don't Be Modest When doing these self-reviews, for the most unknown and idiotic of reasons, they ask the employee to identify areas of improvement and areas of weakness. I'm sure if every employee were honest, it would look something like this:

- I take an hour lunch instead of a half-hour.
- Find ways to come in on time and not 30 minutes late, and getting away with it by sneaking in through the back door.
- Spend less time surfing the Web and more time actually doing the work assigned to me.
- Balance the use of time on Facebook and Pinterest on my smartphone, which the boss cannot monitor, and become a more productive employee in the workplace.
- The first 45 minutes could be better used answering e-mail received overnight than by spending it in the break room making my morning cup of coffee, microwaving my pastry, filling up my water bottle, and talking over the water cooler about last night's reality talent show.
- Avoid becoming immersed in the latest corporate action rumor taking place as if I actually have a role in it or will in any way benefit from it.

- Avoid spreading false layoff rumors just to see others get worked up into a tizzy.

If what we really thought could actually somehow have positive effects on our career, then this particular section on our reviews would be helpful. But it is not. So do what every Edward and Debbie in the workplace does and embellish your strengths through your weaknesses.

Personally, I demonstrated my strengths by answering the corny "weakness" questions as "Not Applicable to Employee" or "None to Date" or my favorite: "To Be Determined." I am sure that the boss man didn't appreciate my borderline narcissistic personality that came through on my reviews, but most bosses do not care enough about it to ask you to revise it after they submit it, because it requires them to wait yet again for the changes to be made and the effort and the confrontation of asking for it to be changed.

The response might not have improved my standing in the short term, but at least I didn't have to give legitimate areas for improvement only for it to be held against me in the future through my own admission.

So you may not like my own personal approach to the no-win questions found on reviews, but whatever you decide, do not be honest about your weaknesses. That's what the "Garys" and "Larrys" of the workplace do, and it leads them to a life of being stepped on and always being nothing more than the tools of the "Edwards" and "Debbies."

In the Boss Man's Hands Because the reviews that nearly all companies undergo are pointless in nature, the boss man finds ways to make the process easier by finding as many ways as possible to not exert strain on a single brain cell when the reviews submitted have to actually be, well, "reviewed."

By doing so they create what the corporate world likes to call "process improvements." It's the corporate code word for "laziness." By the time my last year on the job rolled around, they had most of our questions categorized into a system that functioned at the kindergarten level. If you performed at a high level, you received a "green" rating. If performance was just average, you were "yellow," and the employee who was ready to be thrown on the ash heap of corporate unemployment received the "red" rating.

Then it was determined that so many individuals were being ranked as a "green," a committee board decided after a long-drawn out internal review that another color had to be added. For the exception—that is, your name is "Edward" or "Debbie"—you received the magical "blue" annotated for the questions and overall review. On my own personal reviews, of course, I gave myself a "blue" for every category, question, and overall rating as well.

It's essential that you always do, at the least, enough to keep your job, and I encourage everyone to make sure they are doing the best work they possibly can. But, in the end, you cannot serve two masters. If you want to be a successful trader, you will have to decide how much less successful you'll want to be in your corporate jobs.

When I went on trips with others, and at night when everyone went downstairs to drink and be merry, it would have been nice to join them. I could have gotten in good with not only the boss man but also the boss man of the boss man. So you would think I would be motivated to mingle with these folks, but I did not. I was a recluse. I stayed in my hotel room, flipped on the television to whatever was on for some background noise, and plugged away on my research and other trading activities that were required of me to ensure that I could continue successfully in my ultimate goal of leaving the corporate stratosphere for full-time trading.

Making the transition from part-time trader to full-time trader requires significant choices and sacrifices along the way. In some ways it will feel like you are doing a kamikaze on your future growth as an employee, but ultimately that is not what you want here anyway. If you get promoted along the way, that is great as well and nothing to feel guilty about. However, do not expect the corporate world to still endear themselves to you when you no longer accept them as your first love (though they should still be your first responsibility).

Seeking Out Increased Responsibility versus Effective Trading

Done with your responsibilities for the day, week, or month? That is great! The normal tendency is to go to the boss man and let him know that you do not have any more work to do and he should give you more assignments to complete.

But I would not do that.

More Work = Difficult Trading

I would let those assignments come to me. Often when you are done with your work and you go to your boss asking for more, he or she may find it appropriate to call on one of your busier colleagues like Edward, Debbie, Gary, or Larry, who live their lives biting off more than they can possibly chew, and shovel off some of their workload onto you. In the corporate world, this is tagged with the fancy label of *offloading*.

Work Never Gets Back to Normal That's fine if you work in a vacuum, but what happens when your other job responsibilities pick up and you have to take care of those assignments as well as the ones that were offloaded on you. Essentially, you'll have a far greater workload that will inevitably get in the way of your trading, and if it does not, you will become known to the boss man through others complaining about your work performance because you were unable to get their work done for them.

Remember, the best thing as a trader is to be all caught up on your work. It is the perfect scenario. How can your boss get mad at you for doing your job? This is where you are much better able to place a greater focus on your trading endeavors without having to worry about compromising your work performance in the process.

Promotion Competition There were a few times where I was promoted while I was in Corporate America. There were only so many people that could get promoted each year. In fact, it was so crazy that they would rank their employees. Only the top employees from each department were promoted. But if you were getting promoted too quickly, then you would get knocked down lower because they did not want you to get too many promotions in too short a time period.

Let's say there were three promotional spots for a given fiscal year, but there were five people who worked hard enough to deserve being promoted. They would have to decide which three out of the five would receive the promotion, and the Edwards and Debbies would debate over who would receive the promotion, where only the three favorites would actually realize what they deserved.

The problem with this mentality is that it creates some stiff competition 365 days out of the year among employees. Despite the organization's being so hell-bent on teamwork, they manufactured a corporate jousting arena for employees to prioritize their time by trying to knock the other off their horse as many times as possible so that come promotion time, they would be the ones getting a higher level tagged to their job title when promoted. Immersing myself in that mindset and environment just never carried much appeal to me.

Broad-Based Mindset This corporate mentality isn't unique to where I came from; instead, it is quite prevalent among large companies. It has its roots in one of today's biggest industry tycoons, who reshaped the workplace during his tenure as chief executive officer (CEO) of one of America's largest corporations. Because of his apparent success in managing people, zealous CEOs across the country decided they needed to foster a similar environment to the one I have described so far.

Endless Competition I realized that unless I laid my trading habits aside, there was no way I was going to be able to compete with these people by simply working an eight-hour shift each day. The folks who got promoted would volunteer for the hard assignments, work the long hours, and then brown-nose any individual that was one or more levels higher than they were. If you were their equal, then beware—you were not even safe in their presence with a plastic knife lying around.

Just when they would all get promoted and I would think I was next in line for the promotion and the raise that comes with it, a whole new flock of employees who had been promoted from below me to my current level would be willing to make the same sacrifice all the other employees that went on before me were willing to make.

There's no doubt that I could have competed with them—remember, I *was* employee of the year and that once "rising star" that quickly fell from the heavens. However, had I chosen to enter into the rat race with everyone else to try and be the next Edward, it is unlikely I would have ever found my way into full-time trading.

Finding a Way Despite the Adversity

With that decision came family pressures as well. If you are the breadwinner of the family like I was, coming home and telling your spouse that you are only going to do what is expected and not go above and beyond for your employer (i.e., marrying yourself to the job as well) will undeniably cause stress in your relationship, and you certainly do not want to do that.

I also want to make sure that you don't take me wrong and think that you should slack off on your job, not take it seriously, and be willing to risk getting fired as a result, because that is definitely not what I am saying here. I am simply stating that you have to put your job in the category of a temporary solution to a long-term fix.

Ultimately, you want to be a trader. But in order to trade and get better at doing so, you need a stream of income because numerous mistakes in trading will be made along the way, as well as the simple fact that if you are still working, you have not earned enough income to be that full-time trader. It is a delicate balance—if it weren't, I would not be writing this book. I tried many different approaches to my job. Some worked very well and others not so much. My task over the next 12 chapters is to dig in deep on each of these topics for your benefit—both failures and successes.

The Job Is a Trading Asset

You job is important and, above all else, you have to keep it. While the desire is to eventually migrate into trading full-time, you have to treat your job as a component of your trading. No job means you will have no trading career. When you ultimately make that switch to full-time trading, you have to do so in such a way that you are not putting an undue burden on yourself and also your family in order to succeed.

The worst type of trader is the one who has to make a certain dollar amount each month (or else) to pay the bills, feed the family, and pay the tuition. When that happens, everything goes down the drain. Marriage suffers, emotions are strained, money is absent, and success in trading and thereby bigger profits than before becomes a near impossible task at which few can succeed.

Every dollar from your paycheck that you can put away toward savings or into your brokerage account for additional trading power, you should consider as a winning trade. It is profits that bring you closer to realizing the opportunity of leaving and becoming a full-time trader. So make sure that your job is incorporated into your trading as part of the strategy itself and not two separate items. In doing so, you will keep the necessary perspective of your job, balanced with family pressures, all the while becoming a better and more profitable trader

CHAPTER 4

Don't Quit Your Day Job ... SERIOUSLY!

Continuing the theme of the last chapter, I'd like to share with you my next motivational movie, probably as inspirational as *Rocky, Rudy,* and *Chariots of Fire* combined, and that is *Office Space*.

My favorite scene from the movie occurs when Peter Gibbons, who has completely lost all interest and motivation in his current job, tells the "Workplace Efficiency" job consultants exactly how he feels. In a moment of unabated honesty, Gibbons proceeds to share with the consultants how he uses the side door when coming in late, "spaces out" for the first hour after sitting down at his desk, and repeats those same methods during his extended lunch break.

What really hits at the core of my inner being is when he speaks to the "Bobs" about his inability to be motivated on the job, citing the fact that he works for eight different bosses, and how if he improves the efficiency of the workplace or saves the company a large sum of money, he doesn't see a single dime of what was saved as a result.

And to bring it home he concludes, "So that means that when I make a mistake, I have eight different people coming by to tell me about it. That's my only real motivation is not to be hassled, that and the fear of losing my job. But you know, Bob, that will only make someone work just hard enough not to get fired."

For me it couldn't have been any different.

Just Like the "Real World"

That last statement says it all. When I was still tirelessly working and pushing papers during my first year on the job, I had come up with close to $7 million in negotiated cost savings for my company. Knowing that I had saved the company that much, how do you think that was reflected when consideration for my yearly salary raise came around? Try 3.1 percent on a $30,000 salary. That means I was bumped all the way up to $30,930 per year or $35.76 before taxes for each biweekly paycheck.

No doubt, I felt like my contributions were truly appreciated!

I would have been thrilled with a cut of 0.14 percent of that negotiated savings. That way I could have had a 33 percent raise on a $30,0000 salary, bringing me up to $40,000 on the year, and perhaps I might have been motivated to repeat the same feat next year as well. I wouldn't think that is asking for much—0.14 percent—but, according to the boss man, it most certainly was.

To further my connection with *Office Space*, I pretty much had eight bosses as well. Let me list them:

- *Group lead.* This is the "Larry" who is assigned to micromanage and lean over the shoulder of his employees on a daily basis. This individual has the dreadful job of handling all the management responsibilities that no one else wants to handle.
- *Head contracts manager.* He's the "Gary" who is supposed to be responsible for me, but ultimately just assigns his group lead to bother with me, unless I screw up—then I become his problem, too.
- *Program contracts manager.* The contracts manager on the program I was supporting. Sometimes I supported three or four projects, so you can increase this boss by an equal number, as well as all the ones listed below.
- *IPT manager.* This is an acronym for a fancy job title that stands for integrated project team manager. Essentially, if you are building a wheel, there will be an IPT manager assigned to the spokes, another assigned to the tire, and another assigned to overseeing the air nozzle that attaches itself to the tire. A little bit of overkill, I might add.
- *Project manager.* This field is rife with "Debbies" who just want to flex their muscles and the overall production of that wheel, so that if a significant management role ever comes open, they might be the first person under

consideration to fill that position. So in the process of attaining that goal, they will make your own life a living nightmare. Try to stay out of the crosshairs of this person if you can.

- *Project engineer.* Very similar to the project manager, but instead this person provides the technical support and all things related to the functionality of the product being developed.
- *Deputy program manager.* This management level you have to watch out for, too. They are your Debbies that cannot seem to get over the management hump and to the top, and typically it is because there is a serious character flaw there.

  Just a rule of thumb: if their job title has "deputy" in it, think of the traditional Barney Fife from *The Andy Griffith Show* who thinks they are more powerful and more important than they really are. They are a pit bull that has to constantly be brought down back to earth by the main person in charge, which takes us to the ultimate boss man.
- *Program manager.* Most of the time you are not going to have to deal with this individual, depending on where you are on the totem pole in the organization. He has bigger fish to fry, so the main objective with him is to fly below the radar.

When I did something wrong that caught his attention, usually it meant that the previous seven people mentioned were already complaining to him about something that I did and were determined to cover their own butts in an attempt to not make themselves look bad. What was even better was if he noticed something wrong without any of the aforementioned seven noticing first. Then the rain really came down.

Making Everyone Happy

Since your job and not your trading is still your first priority, your goal, just as it was in my case, is to make sure that the people we have already discussed are always happy with the work that you are doing. That means that you have to draw the line with how you approach your job and how you deal with those in management. Trying to be the corporate yuppy who still wants to rise through the ranks and get noticed by every Larry, Gary, Debbie, and Edward will be a major undoing of your career. However, not giving a rip about your job and solely focusing on trading will likewise sabotage your job.

Managing the Two

The key is to find that balance between the two. If you are still obsessed with climbing up the corporate ladder, you might as well stop reading here and give the book to the guy in the cubicle next to you who seems miserable in his job and in search of some hope of a better way of life.

But if you are serious about this, then you have to realize you are not going to climb the corporate ladder if you are going to remain serious about trading while in your job. Those who try to actively climb the corporate ladder are not trying to balance two professions at the same time like you are. By trying to keep up with the Edwards you are going to open yourself up to some embarrassing moments as a result of trying to burn a candle at both ends of the tunnel. If you want to act like some sort of Superman on the job, that is fine, but your focus and your obsession has to be your full-time job and nothing else. If you want to be serious about your job and rise to the top, you better lower your aspirations for ever making the transition into a full-time trader.

Listen, I am not against your having aspirations of climbing to the top of the corporate ladder. But you bought this book because you want to eventually transition into becoming a full-time trader or at least manage the load between the desk job and the current part-time trader status you are currently labeled with.

However, to become a trader who can do both successfully, you have to have the time and resources. The roadblock standing in the way of your successfully trading part-time is that pesky Monday-through-Friday eight-plus-hour job you currently have to take account for, and that is what I am here to help you with.

The balance isn't easy, of course, and as you delve into the rest of the chapters in this book, the picture will be cleared up, a sense of direction will be given—how you are able to do both and, most important, how you can be successful at both.

Avoid Goals That Give You a False Sense of Hope

How many times have I seen this happen among traders eager to leave the strains of the corporate world? First and foremost, please, please adhere to what I'm about to write in this section. Many times since launching SharePlanner, when someone has joined our services, they have what is popularly labeled "beginner's luck." A person will come to SharePlanner and begin taking some of the trades that I provide and even some of his own. Most of the time, the risk plans and ways to successfully trade the stock are completely ignored, yet because of this brief and common phenomenon, the trader still seems to do very well, often outpacing my own gains for a brief period of time.

The Unstoppable Trader

While this is taking place, it is absolutely amazing to watch it unfold. This trader just starting off truly believes in his mind that he has found the holy grail of trading. I remember an e-mail in which a certain individual proclaimed that he was never going to lose at a trade again!

That was after he had put together five successful trades and doubled down on two of them, instead of letting the stop losses do their job, placing upwards of 50 percent of his capital on individual trades and even holding through earnings on one of the positions. Through this, he netted a cool 15 percent on his average trade.

His mind was in the clouds, though, as he truly thought he had already arrived as a trader and knew everything he needed to know. However, all he was really able to do was enter a stock symbol and put an order in to buy a stock and another one in to sell it a few days later. The gains that he made off of those five trades were simply the results of what happened in between his two actions of buying a stock through no merit of his own.

Being successful right out of the gate is not something to frown upon. It is what it does to the person and their psychological makeup that is the problem. In fact, when I hear there is a first-time trader in our chat room, I actually get excited because if he follows my trades, I just may be the benefactor of some of his beginner's luck.

All kidding aside, though, this individual typically starts seeing dollar signs. He starts doing the math in his mind about how much money he will be trading with if he can duplicate his efforts each and every time and over the long-term what it might look like for his portfolio, lifestyle, and eventual early retirement from the workforce.

Losing All Logic

Instead of keeping level-headed during his early success, the young "victorious" trader actually takes the proactive approach and makes his very own trading spreadsheet and subsequent "path-to-riches" game plan. In this plan, it shows how after a couple of years of trading and a consistent 10 percent return on each trade, they will be able to retire from the workforce and live happily ever after. The best part is that most of these spreadsheets do not account for losing trades, and instead it is averaged into their winning trading by simply deducting a small dollar amount from his winnings.

I know it sounds crazy reading about it here, but it is actually quite funny what the mind will think up and believe when there are dollars involved, as unbridled hope and optimism can be hard to manage and maintain. I remember when I started getting more familiar and making the transition into part-time trading, the same thing happened to me. I had that great feeling toward my trading early on that led me to believe I was invincible, that the gains would pour in almost every day or at least a few times a week. I created a spreadsheet that had me retiring with well over $5 million in my trading account in just five years.

A typical spreadsheet would look something like Figure 4.1.

So after two months, the user is up 28 percent. Now my first question is always "Where are the losing trades?," and I am left even more baffled by the response, "They are averaged into the spreadsheet." Essentially, the trader (if you can really call them that at this point) is telling me that the losers are more of an afterthought and averaged in with the gains of 10 percent per trade.

By the end of two years they believe that their account will actually look like the one in Figure 4.2 on the premise of the scenario I just laid out.

Not a Chance

To say the least, of all the traders I have met, helped, and coached over the years, I have never seen a single person who has come up with this "game plan" and actually achieve its final outcome, or in this case, a cool $3 million. Instead, those who have tried to game the stock market with this kind of a hokey spreadsheet were left with far less capital than what they started with.

Other traders have come up with spreadsheets or unrealistic goals of making 2 percent per day in their trading. They come up with some quirky system of trading leveraged 3X exchange-traded funds and believe they can hyper-trade them enough throughout the day to make a cool 2 percent on their overall capital *each day!* On the surface they justify their irrational gains over the long term with the belief that somehow 2 percent per day is not

Month 1	Trade	Position Size	% Gained	Dollar Amount	New Portfolio Value.
	Trade 1	$10,000.00	10%	$1,000.00	$101,000.00
	Trade 2	$10,100.00	10%	$1,010.00	$102,010.00
	Trade 3	$10,201.00	10%	$1,020.10	$103,030.10
	Trade 4	$10,303.01	10%	$1,030.30	$104,060.40
	Trade 5	$10,406.04	10%	$1,040.60	$105,101.01
	Trade 6	$10,510.10	10%	$1,051.01	$106,152.02
	Trade 7	$10,615.20	10%	$1,061.52	$107,213.54
	Trade 8	$10,721.35	10%	$1,072.14	$108,285.67
	Trade 9	$10,828.57	10%	$1,082.86	$109,368.53
	Trade 10	$10,936.85	10%	$1,093.69	$110,462.21
	Trade 11	$11,046.22	10%	$1,104.62	$111,566.83
	Trade 12	$11,156.68	10%	$1,115.67	$112,682.50
Month 2	Trade 13	$11,268.25	10%	$1,126.83	$113,809.33
	Trade 14	$11,380.93	10%	$1,138.09	$114,947.42
	Trade 15	$11,494.74	10%	$1,149.47	$116,096.90
	Trade 16	$11,609.69	10%	$1,160.97	$117,257.86
	Trade 17	$11,725.79	10%	$1,172.58	$118,430.44
	Trade 18	$11,843.04	10%	$1,184.30	$119,614.75
	Trade 19	$11,961.47	10%	$1,196.15	$120,810.90
	Trade 20	$12,081.09	10%	$1,208.11	$122,019.00
	Trade 21	$12,201.90	10%	$1,220.19	$123,239.19
	Trade 22	$12,323.92	10%	$1,232.39	$124,471.59
	Trade 23	$12,447.16	10%	$1,244.72	$125,716.30
	Trade 24	$12,571.63	10%	$1,257.16	$126,973.46
	Trade 25	$12,697.35	10%	$1,269.73	$128,243.20

FIGURE 4.1 The Beginning of False Hopes

much to make, but they do not account for the position size, volatility, and their false belief that they will not experience much in the way of losing trades. But let me just say, it is a hokey belief that is far more outrageous than the individual who thinks he can average in his losers with a 10 percent per trade return.

Month 24	Trade 354	$335,308.80	10%	$33,530.88	$3,386,618.83
	Trade 355	$338,661.88	10%	$33,866.19	$3,420,485.02
	Trade 356	$342,048.50	10%	$34,204.85	$3,454,689.87
	Trade 357	$345,468.99	10%	$34,546.90	$3,489,236.77
	Trade 358	$348,923.68	10%	$34,892.37	$3,524,129.14
	Trade 359	$352,412.91	10%	$35,241.29	$3,559,370.43
	Trade 360	$355,937.04	10%	$35,593.70	$3,594,964.13
	Trade 361	$359,496.41	10%	$35,949.64	$3,630,913.77
	Trade 362	$363,091.38	10%	$36,309.14	$3,667,222.91
	Trade 363	$366,722.29	10%	$36,672.23	$3,703,895.14
	Trade 364	$370,389.51	10%	$37,038.95	$3,740,934.09
	Trade 365	$374,093.41	10%	$37,409.34	$3,778,343.43
	Trade 366	$377,834.34	10%	$37,783.43	$3,816,126.87

FIGURE 4.2 **Unrealisitic Trading Goals**

Mind-Numbing Trading

I've always been a firm believer that trading should be boring. Once it starts to get that heart-pounding feeling, and edge-of-your-seat thrilling, you have already lost. The prospect of trading successfully when you have the adrenaline rushing for the six and a half hours while the market is open will create an emotional experience that will leave you near penniless and borderline insane at the end of the day.

Real-World Fantasies

Another shortcoming of traders and particularly those stuck in a desk job is the fantasizing about future wealth—here again another shortcoming of my own as a trader long ago—when a trader begins to think that he is in control of the market and not the other way around, that somehow the market is going to bestow upon him access to sums of unfettered wealth.

Making projections and trying to form-fit the market to your goals, desires, and beliefs for what you want to achieve is one of the worst mistakes a person can make when starting out in trading. The disappointment that will come when the cooling-off period begins and reality sets in will undoubtedly cause carnage to the mental capacity of the trader trying to remain unemotional in his or her approach to trading.

Spreadsheet Trade Management

A downfall in projecting future returns on a market that is every bit as unpredictable day to day as who will become the next winner of the Powerball lottery is where a person manages a trade that will be centered on the spreadsheet itself. Instead of managing what the charts show, the person will be telling himself that he needs to net 10 percent on this trade, and more times than not will let 9 percent in gains turn into a loss simply because he was trying to conform the trade to the story he had created with his very own spreadsheet.

What is even worse is if the individual is coming off of a trade that "needs to be averaged in with the next winning trade," then even the slightest loss will require the trader to make at least 20 percent on the trade before he can sell out of his next position. That is a losing proposition under which no trader can perform. Who knows the excruciating kind of pressure he would be under if he lost two or more trades in a row! So avoid it. Avoid any notion of trying to trade beyond the day that you are currently in and what the market is willing to offer.

Don't Watch the Benjamins

There is no other industry where you can see the compounding of your capital faster than you can count it than when you are on the right side of a trade. Being long on a stock that is squeezing the shorts to cover their positions is an incredible experience, no doubt.

I remember one such occasion, where I was in a training session being taught a new skill for my job. I was paying attention but not quite as much as I should. By the way, if you are ever in a training class at work where there are rows of computers, always take the one in the far back corner if you plan on watching the markets simultaneously. Since most training sessions are mind-numbingly boring, most part-time traders would choose to do so.

The reason for choosing the back of the classroom, away from a door, and in the corner of the room itself, is that you will not have anyone who sits behind you with a clear shot of your monitor. Consequently, you will not have to worry about someone assuming that you are not taking in everything that the presenter has to say.

The Squeeze

Back to the story, though. When I was in this class, they were teaching us Microsoft Excel, and since I was pretty much a pro on all things Excel, particularly after creating my faulty trading/retirement plan years before, I tuned out and watched the markets. At the time, I was trading Smith Micro Software Inc. (SMSI), which was trading at a much higher price than what it is currently trading at the time of this writing. The stock had been idle for days upon days, and I was growing quite weary of it at this point. Then just as the presenter was getting into the meat of the presentation, I witnessed a massive short squeeze get under way, and one that was probably the largest I had been a part of to date. The stock was in the $9s, and then minute bar after minute bar the stock was pushing up 1 percentage point after another.

Within 10 minutes that stock was up nearly 10 percent. I was probably up a cool $1,000, which was far more than what I made in a day while on the job. It is funny, though, because I wanted to fist pump and bang the table in excitement while the presenter continued on in the quiet doldrums of her presentation, but I simply could not do that considering the circumstances. So I painfully kept it to myself.

More Money, More Problems But here was where my flaw was as a trader, and this is a huge issue for many part-time traders as well. That is, instead of managing the trade and the price action and responding accordingly as to whether I should buy, sell, or hold, I instead started counting the dollars and trying to manage the trade based on how much the trade was worth in actual dollars, minus my original total share value.

You have lost the battle if you start counting dollars in your trading, and if I were creating a new trading platform today, I would not let traders view the dollar value or how much money was gained or lost on a trade until they were completely out of it. That is what gets so many traders in trouble. You see, if you are up $500 on an individual trade, you start visualizing what those profits will buy you; perhaps it is an iPad or a need for which you were unsure how you would pay, like a new set of new tires for your car or braces for your son or daughter.

The next step in this faulty trading progression is to tell yourself that if you close the trade right now, you can have the assurance of being able to afford that luxury or item or need. While you might be closing out the trade for noble reasons, it will have drastic long-term consequences on your trading.

Ask yourself how the trading mindset that I have described has anything to do with trading stocks and having a valid reason to close the trade and lock in the profits you were holding. The simple answer is absolutely nothing! That is why watching the profit/loss column on your trading platform could not be more wrong for you. It will ensure that you remain emotionally based in your trading and decision making. In fact, the very notion of comparing your gains on a trade to what it would allow you to personally acquire if you were to close the trade out now is by its own definition "emotional trading."

Focus on the Trade Only There is a big difference, though, in what I am speaking of versus being oblivious to the losses you might be piling up and refusing to acknowledge or being aware of a certain flaw in your trading technique. If you are piling up loss after loss, it will be pretty obvious, and not doing anything about it will be even worse. What I am trying to pontificate is not to become absorbed with the dollar aspect of the trade. Stay focused on the percentage gained or loss. Watch the price action and what it is trying to tell you. If the stock requires that you book the gains because it cannot break through resistance, then sell it. If you are short a stock and the prospect of a short squeeze is becoming increasingly possible, then consider taking some of the position off and tightening the stop loss on the rest. This is the way we are supposed to trade, not holding on a stock that you are up \$1,000 on and hoping for \$2,000, simply because you "need" that money and cannot settle for less.

The same can be said when you are on the losing side of a trade. For instance, if you are losing on a trade, and for good reason you placed your stop loss on the trade 5 percent below where you entered the price, you may panic if the trade goes against you, as many traders do. Let's say that a trader is down 4 percent on a trade on a \$10,000 position. He will look at that \$400 loss and panic once he realizes that it is a month's worth of groceries or a car payment. In order to avoid making the trade worse for himself, he will close out the position before giving the stock an opportunity to really play out.

Unless the stock, based on the chart itself, requires that you sell out of your position at a 4 percent loss instead of a 5 percent loss, you are simply trading out of emotion due to the thought or prospect of losing any further capital on the trade. That emotion is quite simply fear, and it, too, can cripple your trading in a permanent way.

The Right Position Sizes

If you are closing out a position based on the dollar gains you are seeing or the losses you are experiencing and not basing it on chart and price movement, you are trading out of emotion, and those emotions are lulling you into the false sense of hope that you are trading for all the right reasons, and that you took the actions that you did for noble reasons. However, the true problem underlying this behavior and the emotionally based decisions it is driving you to make is not because of the dollars at hand being made or lost; rather, it is the size of the position. So if you are watching the dollars far too much, realize that you are probably trading with a dollar amount per trade that is probably too much for you to handle on a steady and consistent basis.

Your money is emotional. What you do with your money is often based on an emotion of what you "feel" that you need, want, and desire. The problem with the stock market is that there is no room for any of that if you wish to be successful as a trader. The less important the dollars are to you, the better you will become as a trader. Far too often, people trade beyond what they can afford to lose, and if that is the case, no matter how well you understand technical or fundamental analysis, you will more than likely not make it in the long term. I am strongly opposed to trading with life savings, loan proceeds, college funds, or anything else that you think you will need the money for at a future date. The less important to your future the capital you are trading with becomes, the better it will be for your overall trading.

Case in point: have you ever wondered why paper trading (i.e., trading stocks without any monetary risk) is so much easier than when you finally go live and actually start trading with your own money? Simply, it is because what you are trading with (i.e., fake money) does not make you feel any emotion, worry, or excitement, and that is because nothing is really at risk. Throw in your own hard-earned money and the wheels will really start to come off the bus. Money and our attachment to it is usually what stands between us and profitable trading.

Position Sizes Dictate Emotional Depth Let's dig a little deeper into this discussion because it is truly paramount that you understand the position sizes when trading and how it will affect your demeanor in the workplace if you do not understand the implications of trading with position sizes that are too large.

The bigger the better when it comes to trading stocks:

Big returns = Big money
Big portfolio = Big positions
Big positions = Big profits
Bigger positions = Bigger cash returns on small percentage gains = Less need for significant winning trades

Why Don't We All Just Trade as Big as We Can? Because the exact opposite is true when you lose and the true reality of the above statements really becomes:

Big returns = Don't come as easily
Big portfolio = Increased anxiety
Big positions = Big losses
Bigger positions = Bigger cash losses on big percentage losses = More need for significant winning trades

What Do We Do Then? Evaluate yourself:

Question: Are you afraid to hold a position overnight, even though you find yourself to be a swing trader?

Answer: Then you are trading too big.

Question: Are you scalping with big positions and settling for pennies on the dollar and finding some satisfaction with it?

Answer: Then you have too much fear in your trading, and you are trading too big.

Question: Are you checking your positions incessantly every minute of every day and getting emotional on small pops a stock might have during normal trading activities?

Answer: Then you are trading too big.

Question: Are you becoming moody at night with the wife/husband/friends/kids and checking futures when you should really be sleeping?

Answer: Then you are trading too big.

What Should I Do? Sounds extreme? It isn't. A lot of people will read this and relate to the large majority of the questions I have asked here. But take some time after the market has closed or during the weekend and really ask yourself, with your average position sizes, what kind of angst and stress is it causing you? If you are watching the profit and loss on your active trades more than the actual price movement of the stock itself, then you probably need to take a step back from trading and figure out how much you need to reduce the position size of your trades.

You may say, "But I won't make as much money." But you won't lose as much either, and the goal here is not how rich you can get off of the market (the fool's draw to trading) but how you can equalize your emotions toward the capital that you trade in such a way that the trading you undertake is close as possible to emotionless (since we are humans, getting rid of the emotions altogether is impossible, despite what others might claim). If you do this, the profits will take care of themselves.

Because you are trading with reduced position sizes, you will likely see your returns go up as you are not making as many mistakes and bad decisions in your trading and are able to trade with less stress and less fear and anxiety.

So, going forward, ask yourself, "How much do I need to reduce the size of my trades before I feel comfortable and near stress free with my trading?" When you find that answer, then that is what you need to trade with. If you reduce your position sizes and still feel the anxiety that came with trading before, then reduce it again . . . and again . . . and again until you find that desired state.

At the end, if you do this, I believe you'll be glad you did. For most, this will not be an acceptable course of action to take because excuses and reasons why they can't do it will block them from making the right decision and they will continue to flounder in their trading. If there is a reason for why you can't trade at a reduced stress level and *must* trade position sizes with which you are not at all comfortable, then there is probably a very, very good reason why you should not be trading at all.

■ Jeopardize Your Trade Before You Jeopardize Your Job

One thing to remember in your job is that you are being paid to perform a set of responsibilities and you should do them well. That goes without saying. I say that because far too often it is easy to get caught up in the trade and do something stupid that will put at risk the job that you need more than the trading itself.

Job Is Priority Number One

If you find yourself in a trade that you know you cannot manage without heavy emotions, pressing time constraints, or not meeting the responsibilities of your normal job (hate it or love it, it is still your current job), then you need to skip that trade. Trade in a way that doesn't affect the psyche or your ability to do what the job mandates you do. A successful trade is not worth much if its profitability results in your standing in the unemployment line.

The key here is to ensure that your job and your trade align with each other. That is what I dedicate the rest of this book to. Trying to be a day trader and an air traffic controller isn't going to mesh. Scalping stocks for small gains while you are supposed to be on foot doing security detail at your local mall is not going to work either. And if sudden changes to your day can happen at a moment's notice (e.g., a firefighter), then placing trades that won't go radically against you at a moment's notice is preferable.

The key is to find the optimal combination between the time that your job affords you to, well, do things not so much related to the job, and the time that your trading strategy requires of you. You can be a successful trader with minimal time spent observing the markets. If your job allows you to have much more time than the normal job to conduct personal affairs or to have downtime, then your trading frequency can be much greater as a result.

Essentially, what is true about the job that you hold should be the opposite of how you trade. Time-consuming job responsibilities means a trading strategy that requires you to be more hands off with your trading. Less time sensitivity and a job where you have the ability to work at your own pace without daily deadlines or a micromanaging boss allows you to customize a trading strategy that allows for higher-frequency trading.

Three Parameters to Account For

Now it is important for you to make sure that the job requirements and trading strategy you employ mesh well with your personality and your ability to trade close to emotion free on the trading parameters and plan that you set for yourself. So you have three parameters to account for: (1) job requirements, (2) time allotted to focusing on trading, and (3) the ideal trading strategy that best coincides with your personality and risk appetite.

If all three of these factors are not accounted for, then your trading will be a miserable failure.

However, by incorporating all three factors, you will position yourself for trading successfully, while managing a full-time job and maintaining good rapport with coworkers as well as finding yourself able to keep the emotions of the trade and worries that come with it from spilling over into your full-time job.

I managed to pull it off managing a high-stress job with my own particular trading strategy. But I did it without a road map and, as a result, had to do a lot of trial and error. If I was able to do it as an individual who is fallible and prone to screw-ups, I am quite confident you will be able to do the same. Much of what I'm about to teach you and the tips I provide come from my own shortcomings as a trader, and despite my setbacks, I exhibited a constant willingness to push forward and find a better way. Equipped with the content of this book, there is no doubt your path to becoming a full-time trader can become much less stressful and much more likely than the odds that I faced of shedding the restraints of Corporate America and becoming the full-time trader that I am today.

CHAPTER 5

The Essentials to Your "Workplace Trading Desk"

Oh, it seems like yesterday, the office roulette game. Your office was yours until someone above you became desirous of it. For most individuals it works like this: the bigger the office, the more prestigious, the better you feel about yourself, and the more highly someone might think of you. It is really superficial when you think about it.

I benefitted, at least for the purposes of this book and my being able to explain it to you, from working in any and every kind of office work environment. If you can think of it, I have been there. From having my own office to shared offices, to desks in the hallway, and even a desk in the middle of a common area surrounded by seven other offices that had direct access to see at any given time what was on my computer screen. I've been in the cubicle environment and even in settings with two or three people crammed into one cubicle area—awkward, to say the least.

Environmental Trading

One thing worth noting right away is that you have to adjust to your environment. If you work at a company that prides itself in musical offices, then you need to have a basic game plan that will allow you to adjust to any setting or circumstance. Just to reiterate what I said in the opening paragraph, while it is nice to have a large office, it is not likely to last, because if you like it and find it spacious and fitting for all or most of your needs, then there is likely someone at a higher pay grade that will think the same as well and will act on obtaining it from you.

Office Squares

The boss man, where I came from, had it laid out that your level corresponded with the number of tiles on the ceiling (you know those square tiles that are about 2.5 feet by 2.5 feet). Entry or clerical folks were not technically allowed to have offices until all those over them had acquired their offices, and if you were a Level B, you were entitled to an office, but one without a door, most certainly without a window, and that office could have only eight full tiles or fewer on the ceiling. However, if office space was limited, you were required to take a cubicle, share an office (up to four people in one office), or possibly reside in a cubicle with just as many people. Often, there were ways around it, but that was only good until someone became interested in where you were staying. Squatter's rights meant nothing!

I had one office where there were probably 25 ceiling tiles and even included my own conference table. How long do you think I kept that office? Try a month. They not only moved me out of the office but out of the building into a dingy 50-year-old building that smelled of rotten cheese and mold.

Go Small

I would later come to realize that the key to keeping your very own office was to have the worst office possible. If you were afforded the choice between a very plush office and one that was just a little bit larger than a broom closet, I would recommend choosing the latter. Why is that, you say? Consistency, longevity, and continuity. If you constantly pick out the best office, you will constantly be finding a new office, too. Your objective is not to gain glory or look special or have some kind of air of prestige associated with your name. No, it is to trade in such a way that you can eventually leave the workplace, or at the very least successfully trade part-time as a full-time employee.

Take the office that nobody wants, and when it comes time to reshuffle the office space, you will not be at the top of the pecking order for removal.

In fact, if you pick a dingy enough office, it may keep you where you are while others above you are relegated to the cube farm. They might just be glad that someone was willing to occupy the office you were in.

How to Lay Out Your Office

Often, we cannot choose the office we eventually come to call our second home. It is usually forced upon us. With that said, I am going to go over the most common office setups and how you can survive trading in the most undesirable of conditions.

Figure 5.1 shows a simple office layout where the desk is strategically placed in front of the door. Do not put the desk against the back wall as some may do, because curious eyes will always take a glimpse at what is on your computer screen. So don't even think about putting your desk up against the wall and in plain sight for all to see.

Figures 5.2 and 5.3 show some other acceptable office layouts, for various circumstances, including offices you share with others.

Figure 5.4 is similar to the first design, but this time you have the door in the middle of the office. You will want to tilt the monitor by placing it at the closest corner of the desk and closest to the door as well.

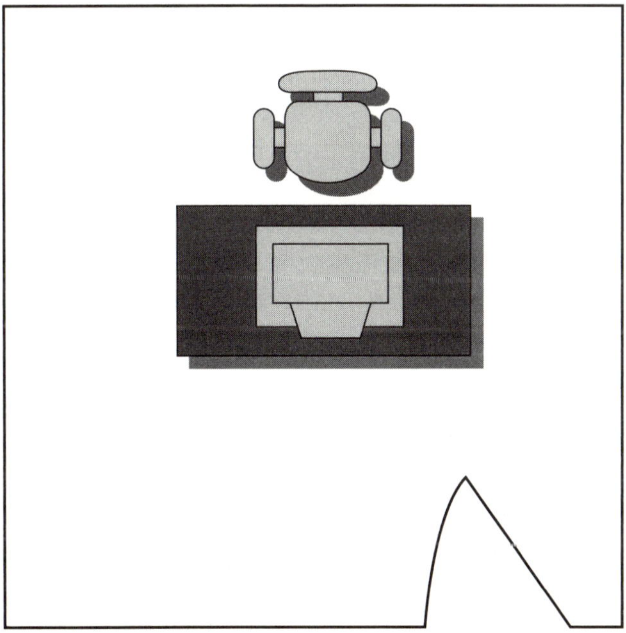

FIGURE 5.1 **A Basic Office Layout**

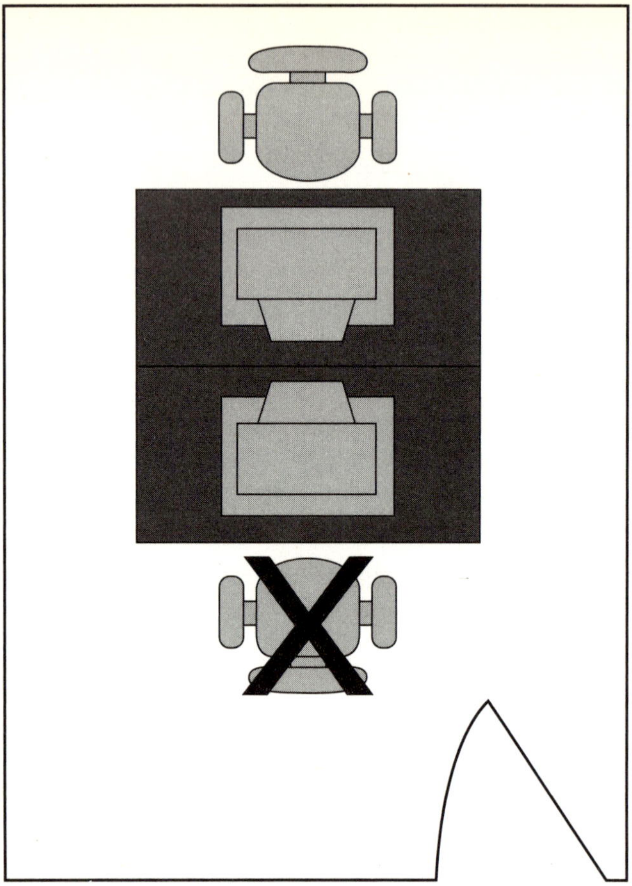

FIGURE 5.2 **Do Not Put Your Back to the Door**

You must avoid taking the desk nearest the door, but if someone claimed that location for their own, then you have no choice but to move the desk to where it is more privacy friendly as well as being easier work with (see Figure 5.5). It is not perfect, and it does put your new office mate somewhat in the line of vision of your monitor, but if you keep your body in front of the computer monitor, then you should avoid giving them a clear shot of it. Besides, the employee sitting behind you has to be focused on his screen and would have to perch his head over his own monitor to view yours.

Finally, if you have side-by-side desks; if you are farthest from the door, tilt the monitor away from the door as shown in Figure 5.6. This desk is your first choice. If you do not get this workspace, then make sure to align your monitor accordingly for seat two.

FIGURE 5.3 Another Simple Layout

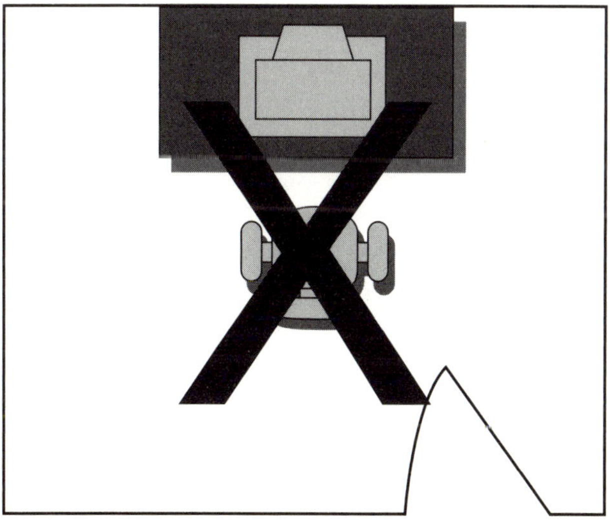

FIGURE 5.4 Layout Mistake

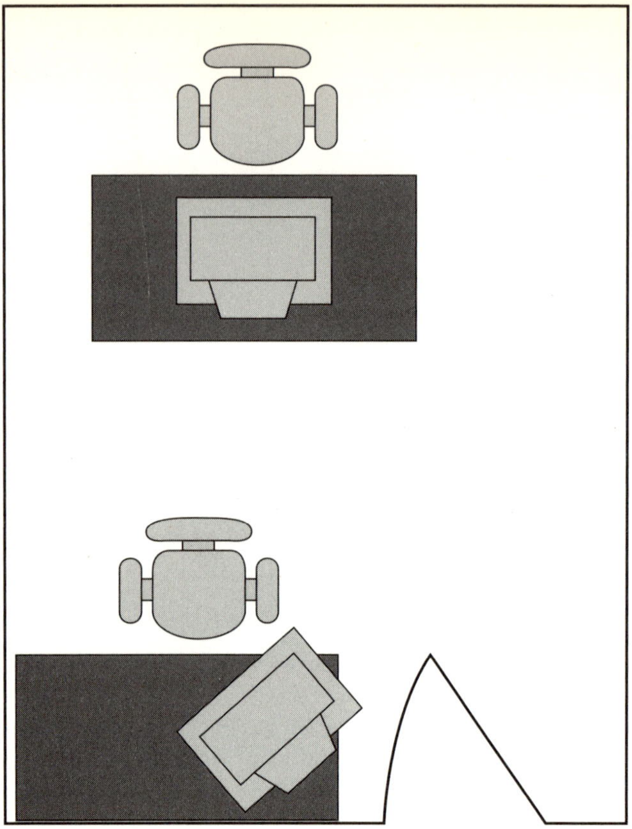

FIGURE 5.5 Complex Layout if Necessary

The final layout (Figure 5.7) deals with office sharing in a more square setting than the rectangle versions we were dealing with. Either one of these desks is worth taking. The only thing you do not want to do is to place your desk at the far end of the room and away from the door. If that is the case, you cannot avoid having your screen monitored by everyone who walks by. Between the two shown, I would choose the first one because of the way the door opens and the ability to keep your screen private.

The goal for all of these layouts is privacy. Arrange the desk and the location of your monitor based on the desire to keep your computer screen private if the boss man strolls into the office and from those who are passing by. Perception in the workplace is everything, and a lot can be falsely assumed by what is seen in just a moment on your work desk. So keep them from guessing its contents at any given time by being more strategic with your workplace layout.

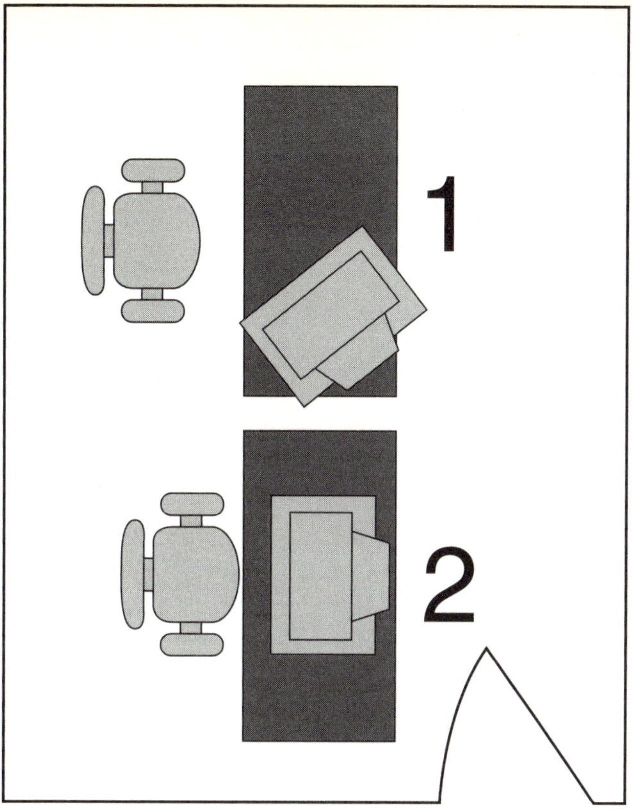

FIGURE 5.6 Side-by-Side Layout

Working with the Computer that You Are Given

A big chunk of this chapter pertains to dealing with matters that you really cannot do anything about. Whether it is the office space you are dealt or the computer you are assigned, the important part is that you adjust appropriately to the circumstances you are given.

Unless you are a company like Apple, or Google, or some of the more tech-savvy organizations out there, it seems to be a rule of thumb that the bigger the company, the more outdated their hardware is. Twelve years after its initial release, there are still plenty of large companies that are running on Internet Explorer 6. That's right, a browser that Microsoft no longer supports, and is probably compatible with only a quarter of the existing web sites out there, or at least that has been the case from my own experience.

FIGURE 5.7 Multiperson Office Setting

I find that browsers that are far more developed, faster, and web site friendly like Google Chrome or Mozilla Firefox are ignored in large part by Corporate America.

Desktop versus Laptop

Obviously, it is important to have a respectable computer setup. The more control you have over this, the better. While I do not recommend laptops for full-time traders, they are ideal for part-time traders in the workplace. They give you all the needed flexibility for staying up on your trades, whereas a desktop computer limits you to having access to your brokerage account only when you are in the office (smartphones and tablets will be discussed later). Here is another aspect of Corporate America that I simply do not understand: laptops are comparable in costs to desktops, yet most companies still act like having a laptop is some sort of luxury item.

Filling Out the Request Form Where I come from, the information technology (IT) department, which handles all PC issues, made us fill out a five-page form to justify the assignment of a laptop to us—seriously! We had to state how much business travel we would be doing on average, explain why we needed the laptop while traveling (because I am not going to bring my own computer!), why our position required the laptop, and just about every other duplicative question that can be asked but only answered the same way each time.

Essentially, you need to fill out this form with as many buzzwords as you can possibly think up. I used expressions like "synergies gained with increased flexibility," "cross-function efficiencies," and, my personal favorite, "an integrated solution to my workplace environment that will provide ideal communicative abilities with organizational stakeholders that we seek to deliver customer value in a results-oriented operation." Please feel free to use these on your own questionnaires in attempt to get that golden laptop. Who knows, management might be so "turned on" by your grasp of the corporate vocabulary that you may get a raise out of it.

Oh, and of course, there is the management approval that is required with just about everything associated with your job outside of urinating and breathing. For some, the boss man will be hard to convince. He will try to question your grasp of the buzzwords you used in your justification form, out of fear that somehow you might have a better handle on the corporate vocabulary. That is why going with what I laid out above will overwhelm them to the point that they will avoid engaging you too much on the matter out of fear that they appear inadequate on the level of corporate-speak that you have shown them in the justification form.

Ideally, the management approval will be more of a formality before it is sent on to the IT department.

The Laptop Luxury Another advantage to having a laptop over a desktop is, of course, its portability. I remember numerous occasions where I would get called into an unexpected meeting. Well, what would you do if there was a position you had on at that moment? The job, of course, comes first and you have to go to the meeting (unfortunately).

With the laptop you can take your trade with you. Also, it looks impressive to a boss when you sit in a meeting that most of the time (at least in my case) you have no reason for attending, but you look the part of someone who is hard at work. The fact of the matter was that I was in a meeting that had no direct ties to me, but because people were so obsessed on being a team, I still got dragged into it. In particular, the broad project meetings where you had some 30 different job functions present giving a "status" on their work often led to my immediate zone-out. I could care less what 29 other job functions were doing. Why would I be the least bit interested in what they are doing when I can barely stand what it is that I am doing in my own job function?

Getting through Meetings I could not leave the meeting because, of course, that would show publicly the disinterest for everyone else's status that I privately harbored. So having a laptop handy allowed me to get through these grueling "team-building" moments. Using a laptop during meetings, as long as you are not expected to chime in at all, looks productive, like you have pressing matters that must be addressed and you are squeezing every bit of efficiency out of meetings and the time at work you have to do your job.

On the contrary, if you were in a meeting, you were doing your job because that was where they wanted you to be at that point in time. If they wanted you to continue with your workload, they should have left you in the office, which is what they chose not to do. So I am completely at peace with whipping out the laptop, in the moments that I'm not needed to be cued in to what is being discussed so that I can watch the market, find new trade setups, or simply check the latest scores on ESPN, because most people in these meetings are simply wanting to be heard without any true intrinsic value attached to what they are actually saying. There is always that one person (or two, or three, or fifteen) who is far too comfortable with the meeting, and those in the room, when called upon to talk about issues, seem as though they are opening some kind of diary, or better yet, reading the status updates they published to Facebook over the past week.

The whole purpose of these meetings is futile to begin with. If you truly have a pressing need, you are not going to wait until the meeting at hand to announce it to everyone; you'll e-mail or address the people at their office. So you get 30 people in there and the meeting lasts an hour and 20 minutes, you have collectively wasted a week's worth of productivity equal to one person among your entire group. That is asinine.

Now you know why I like the laptop and why it is so crucial to the job. If you do not get a laptop and you are stuck in these senseless meetings, do not go whipping out the smartphone in an attempt to try and do the same thing, because more than likely people will think you are clearly doing something nonrelated to company work—either playing *Farmville* or sexting with Anthony Weiner.

Additional Advantages Other advantages to having the laptop include travel. If they have you traveling, you have a perfect gateway to getting them to procure you a laptop. The ability to take the laptop home and do any work that you need to get taken care of, whether work related or stock market related, is a huge advantage.

My last reason is that most companies often will give you administrative rights on your computer, which can go a long way in allowing you to install software (if it doesn't put your job at risk) that might make your limited time as a trader at work more effective. Ideally, installing your brokerage software and their trading platform is a huge advantage to have as a part-time trader. Because you are mobile having the ability to install all the needed software is a great option to have.

Stuck with the Desktop

In the case that you are relegated to just a desktop, and most of the folks in the corporate world usually are stuck with some clunker of a desktop that has not been upgraded since dial-up modems were a fad, you are going to have to plan accordingly. Successful trading as a full-time worker requires being fluid with the circumstances that you are faced with and even adjusting your methods and strategies where it is needed.

Sometimes after trying to do everything in your power to get rid of that desktop and upgrade to the laptop, you have to move forward with the desktop. That means, not using a brokerage, that you cannot regulate the amount of streaming that takes place. It also means you may not be able to trade in such a way that requires on-demand system access and trading at a high frequency.

Making What You Have Better Every boss is different, of course, but if at all possible, constantly be in the ear of your boss and try to get components of your desktop swapped out if there is no chance of landing a laptop. It is hit-or-miss whether your boss will allow for upgraded components on your computer, but the area of upgrade you should focus on is the amount of random access memory (RAM) in the computer (I would aim for at least 8 gigabytes of RAM), which speeds up the efficiency, expands the memory of the computer, and results in faster processing. The next area can often be a harder area to receive an upgrade in, but that would be the processor itself. I'd stick with Intel processors, and try to get as close as possible to the best that there is.

If there is no support on your end to provide you with a computer that works for you, simply let the computer die. Do not maintain it, do not keep it up. All computers die anyway; if they are making you work on one that is on life support, then pull the plug and let it die a natural death.

When I was trading off of my desktop at work, I was relegated to a desktop that had a performance of less than 300 MHz on the processor. That was incredibly slow, even for that time. While those types of computers cannot even function in today's computing environment, even just 10 years ago, that computer was severely hampered in its performance capabilities. I was new on the scene and no one really seemed to care that I was using a computer that was absolutely useless. Not only that, but they still expected me to perform on the same level as the person in the next cubicle over, who had the latest and greatest computer. That simply is not possible to do in today's digital age.

Instead of doing normal performance maintenance that is quite normal on the computer, I was reluctant to defragment the hard drives, look for malware, and so on. Usually, I would turn off the sleep mechanisms and just let that computer run around the clock. Eventually, that computer would die out and as a result I would get a desktop system comparable to that of my peers and be able to work with as much efficiency as they did.

Web-Based Trading Often, the desktop platform restricts employees from installing their own software, which essentially eliminates a number of your higher-end trading platforms. Most companies will not give you administrative rights on your computer unless it is explicitly approved by management. As a result, you'll find that there are a handful of platforms that are strictly software based that you will not want to use for your trading system because you will not have sufficient administrative rights to install them on the desktop.

That means you will want to use a Web-based trading platform. I use TDAmeritrade's platform via ThinkorSwim. For most of my trading career I have been with TDAmeritrade in some way, shape, or form. I left their platform after not being overly happy with their fills, among other things, so I switched over to Thinkorswim, which was later acquired by TDAmeritrade (which I obviously was not overly thrilled about). I have stuck it out with ThinkorSwim, despite their being acquired by the brokerage I left originally, and I remain content with all that they have to offer, not to mention that you can negotiate your commission rates with them.

The reason I bring this up is that when I was using them while in Corporate America (and long before they were ever acquired), they had a great software platform, but because I had a desktop computer I could never use their software due to the administrative rights issue with installing it on my desktop.

What they did have, though, was a Web-based platform that performed just as well on the fills and real-time quotes as their software version. As a result, I was able to get around the administrative rights issue and simply log in to an online portal and still trade successfully without compromising my trading strategy.

Using Your Smartphones and Tablets as Trading Tools

This has become one of the best developments in technology for traders, and that is not just for entertainment purposes, either. For the working, part-time trader there could not be a better trading asset than the smartphone and tablet. Apple, no doubt, has pioneered this brand new world for traders, which made trading possible, easy, and convenient for the first time in the palm of your hand. In my opinion, this was just as significant as the advent of online trading.

While it is largely agreed that you do not have the same computing power as a desktop, the smartphones and tablets are quickly catching up, and particularly when you compare their capabilities to a laptop. Regardless, these handheld devices open up a world of new opportunities. Because of the size of the screen, it is not as easy to place an order on a smartphone as it is placing it on a desktop per se; however, you cannot take a desktop to a meeting, and you cannot take it on travel, and you can stay connected with your mobile device no matter what kind of corporate roadblocks are put in place.

Social Media and Workplace Trading

I am a huge fan of Twitter and its ability to keep me abreast of the latest market developments and market activities. I am constantly staying updated, and with mobile apps, you do not need to access Twitter or other social media sites on your computer. Instead, the functionality on the mobile devices is comparable to what you have using a desktop browser.

I highly recommend that you follow some of the financial names out there, particularly my own, which is @shareplanner, and others, too, such as @zerohedge, @stocktwits, @slopeofhope, @drudge_report,

@foxbusiness, @bloombergnews, @cnbc, and there are many others as well worth following. In regard to traders and those who provide solid actionable trade ideas, there are a number of those, too, including @sp_trades and @fuinhaz.

In my experience, I have not found there to be a lot of applications for trading when it comes to Facebook, LinkedIn, and other popular forums, but besides Twitter, I also am a huge fan of StockTwits and the real-time social collaboration among traders that, like Twitter, limits the character use, but provides a mobile platform that is extremely useful for developments within stocks, actionable trade ideas, gauging market sentiment, and breaking news for the market at large and individual stocks in particular.

No matter your circumstances as a part-time trader in the workplace, it is not impossible to succeed. Modern technological advancements have made it where you can be as fluid as a river in your approach to trading. Regardless of the barriers that might be put in your way, succeeding as a part-time trader has never before been within your grasp as much as it is today. You cannot expect the organization that you work for to lay out the red carpet for you and provide you with all the tools that you need, but the tools are available outside of them, and you simply need to reach out and take the reins that leads to you trading profitably.

PART II

The Game Plan

Before You Clock In

We all hate it when that early morning alarm goes off. If you are like me, I have to set multiple alarms because I am such a heavy sleeper. If it were a Monday, I was almost certain to clock in late. I could get pretty bitter about the prospect of returning to work on a Monday. In fact, Sundays would more times than not find me in a dour mood because it was the last day of the weekend, and that meant the beginning of another five-day work-week, which always felt like an eternity until Friday came around again.

I became quite the nighthawk simply because going to sleep at night meant a quick passage to the next day of work. Instead of going to sleep at a respectable time like 11 P.M., I would extend my evenings to 1 A.M. or later. That way, I was able to extend my awake time from work by a couple of extra hours.

Your Research Must Be Done

One thing I learned as a trader is that I could not simply just "wing it" with my trading once I got to work. More specifically, I could not do all my premarket research while on the job (that is because I had far more important obligations I was required to address like my starting fantasy football lineups, the latest political scandal on the Drudge Report, and filling out my NCAA Tourney bracket). The time was not there for me to do my premarket research, and I needed to conduct that effort in a distraction-free environment. The confines of my home was the place to do that in order to make sure that I gave myself the best chance at trading successfully during the day ahead.

The premarket research is by far the most important part of a trader's daily routine. Not doing the required work up front is like taking a vacation without bothering to map out how to get to your final destination, or cooking a five-course meal without checking to see first whether you have all the necessary ingredients. In the corporate world it is equivalent to not filling out a "strategic guide plan" before you complete a "process improvement initiative" that allows for you to populate your "weekly activity metric."

In essence, you *must* complete your trading research before you clock in.

A Typical Morning

Out of necessity, I got in the habit early on of waking up at 5 A.M. each morning to prepare for the market session that awaited me that day. I was blogging as well, and that often helped me with my research, to define market conditions in writing rather than try and store away the analysis in the back of my head.

After running through my screens and combing through my actionable trade setups for the day, I would find that it was often extremely difficult to get to work before 7:30 A.M.; having to be at work before 8 A.M. seemed to be some form of cruel and unusual punishment. The only thing worse would be an unpaid internship position.

Start-Time Struggles

I kid you not, it seemed that no matter how efficiently I managed my time studying the markets, I simply could not make it to work by that blasted 7:30 A.M. start time. Obviously, if I did not have to spend a couple of hours each morning putting together my plan for trading each day, I would be able to get there on time. But if I am really honest with myself, if I did not have to do the amount of research starting at 5 A.M. each morning, I'd probably just sleep in regularly until 7 A.M. and then struggle still to be at my desk on time. What is even more amazing is that they actually expected us to be working at full-tilt by 7:30 A.M.

The boss man and that cold-hearted employee manual they gave us when we were hired stated that coffee, water, and "chit-chat" had to be done before the start time. Furthermore, the computer should be booted up and running and we should be "in progress" with the day's current assignments. What were they expecting, though—for all of us to just file in like robots that cannot think, eat, or do anything but company work, simply because we are on company time?

In theory, I might make myself sound like an idiot with that previous statement, but in reality, companies in Western civilization with employees earning salaries with advanced education will face massive employee turnover year after year if they don't allow for subtle office comforts. That means not coming down hard on an employee even though he is a solid contributor, because he decides to check out the box scores on ESPN from last night's baseball games or maybe has a thing for the office secretary and enjoys dropping by her desk for some small talk with higher hopes for the future.

That employee manual was so hated that I could have become somewhat of a cult hero among my colleagues had I made a custom "peeing Calvin" sticker letting loose on that blasted, unsympathetic handbook and stuck it to my office door. But then my plans of seamlessly transitioning from the part-time to the full-time trader would have been thwarted.

Running Late

Often, I would show up to work 20 to 30 minutes late. Sometimes my office location was right near the boss, and other times my office was in a different geographical location or just a different part of the building. Either way, I had my tricks of the trade. There was no way that I could literally wake up earlier, without having to practically go to bed as soon as I got home from work, and as you know from what I wrote about earlier in this chapter, maximizing my evening hours was very important to me. So there was no doubt a certain degree of lateness to my work arrival when you not only have to do all your research in the mornings, but still had to eat breakfast, sometimes get the little buckaroo up and fed, and not forget about getting my own self ready as well. Those two hours each morning before work tended to go by really, really quick.

Parking Is Not as Easy as It Looks When I pulled into the parking lot, there were a number of steps that I would take in order for the boss man to not realize I was arriving late on the scene. First, I would park in a location that was not in direct view of his office window. To do so would be sheer stupidity, but nonetheless a common "rookie mistake" often made by new hires in the workforce.

Let's face it, no matter what you do thereafter during the day, or to conceal your lateness, if you are seen driving into the workplace after the day has started for everyone else, you are done for—toast! Everything you do the rest of the day will be tainted through those lenses of your late morning arrival. Now I actually had some good bosses that actually did not care if I came in late, just as long as I did the job well and did not make them look bad. Those "Garys" got it. They understood how to strike a positive relationship and trust between boss man and employee. But most allow the power they wield to go straight to their head and will cut off their nose to spite their face. If you are a boss man reading this, do not be that guy.

Once you master this simple step, you then proceed to get out of the car. Here, it is important to keep your head on a 180-degree swivel. If you have to swipe a card to get inside the office building, it is important to be aware of any other latecomers that you can trail into the building. But do not make it obvious that you are trying to trail them in. And by trailing I simply mean letting that individual swipe in first, and when he walks in, you just follow in behind him. That eliminates any possibility that you will be electronically snitched on. Sometimes if I noticed a late arrival coming in behind me, I would drop to one knee and start tying my shoe until she passed by me. I would not follow close behind, but just enough so that I knew I would be able to catch the door before it closed on me.

Office Routes The route to your office should be one that avoids all paths that could likely result in your running into your boss. Oh, yes, and another tip. Do not walk in with anything. I mean nothing. I understand that you may have coffee, bags, lunches, purses, and other personal items that are of importance to you, but do not walk into the office the first time in the day with them in tow if you are going to be late.

Leave them in the car, because the key here is to look like you were on time and since the boss man has not seen you from 15 minutes earlier when you were supposed to be at your desk steadily plodding away at the day's responsibilities, you have to give the impression beyond a shadow of a doubt that you have been there all along and he just had not run into you until now. So leave the personal effects in the car, at least until you've been seen by those who "matter."

Printer Friendly Now, if you want to personally touch it up some, do what I did when I went about it as I tried to win an Oscar for my dramatization of the on-time employee (by the way, add a little drama to my storyline in this book, and you have a great made-for-TV series ready for primetime viewing). Find the printer not in your department or outside in the hallways and go there first before going to your office. Grab a couple of sheets of paper off of the printer and start walking down the hallway with them in hand. You can also accessorize this look by actually bringing in the cup of coffee that you left in the car. But when you walk in, with the papers in hand, you will want to look deeply at those pages. It is preferable that you have some content on those pages as well.

Most of the time printers are chock-full of abandoned printouts that people forgot to pick up from days ago or they were simply just too lazy to go and get them. Target those as your props for appearing on time. If you can find some of those wide 11-by-16 printouts, it is even better. That is when people know you've really got your act together because you will probably have some crazy flowcharts and metrics and other material that moistens the tastebuds of upper management.

So with your coffee in the left hand and your printouts in the right hand, just casually stroll into your department, sipping on the coffee but not taking your eyes off of the printouts in hand. A little talking to yourself that registers slightly higher than a mumble really sells your "timeliness." No one will think for a moment that you are just now walking in. Then, to just bring it home, drop your hand that is holding the pages down to your thigh so that the pages make a noise of their own, throw your head back, and say something to the effect of "Not again . . .," "They still didn't add the quality inspection into the process like they were supposed to," or my personal favorite (combo-style): "Dadgum, those slackers left it out again. I guess we are just going to have to schedule a status meeting to address this and make sure we have the necessary accountability metrics in place next time." Instead of hearing a "You're late," you'll instead hear sympathy in the form of "What now," "How can I help," and so on. Your response only needs to be, "No, no, nothing you can do, I just expect others to be as passionate about their job as I am."

Let me just say that if someone hears you say that kind of stuff, or if you have a document in hand that you just happened to swipe off of the neglected pile of printout rejects, no one is going to question if you are late or that you spent the last two hours at home researching and planning your trading session that will commence in the next couple of hours.

Prideful Management

Use technology to your benefit. Sell yourself as being sold out to your company, even though every bone in your body longs for the full-time trading career. In reality, this does not just apply to traders but to anyone looking to escape the rigors of the corporate world. Some people love it, and good for them; I applaud them for it. But I was never really cut out for all the nonsense that goes into a job where you are better known by your company as a series of digits on your employee badge rather than by your actual first and last name.

Despite that, I could play the game to my own benefit better than anyone. Had I truly taken a liking to my job and had a desire to move up the ladder with the Edwards and Debbies, I most certainly would have done well at it, but in doing so I felt like I would cheapen my own self-worth by humiliatingly having to be almost worshipful of the CEOs, CFOs, managers, and directors alike.

Despite my belief and our Founding Fathers' beliefs that all men are created equal, it does not play out that way in the corporate world. Do not fool yourself—most CEOs have such an elevated view of themselves that they feel the need to separate themselves from the crowd, with special parking spots, private dining rooms, and their own personal bathroom, just so they don't have to intermingle with the commoners.

I was definitely a company guy but for my own personal reasons. I wanted out. That was the long-term solution, but in order achieve that, I had to sell myself as the ideal employee in the short term so that I could realize my own personal dreams and desires.

Delayed E-mails

One way I played the role of the ideal employee was through various and subtle nuances. If you think about it long and hard, there are plenty of ways you can do this in different forms and versions of what I write about throughout the pages of this book. Get familiar with the delayed e-mail. When the company let out at 5 P.M., and it was 4:55 P.M. and I was still typing up a personal e-mail, I didn't send it out at 4:57 P.M. No way! That just looked like I was just trying to get something out the door before I walked out of the office at the earliest time allowed under company rules. Instead, I would use my e-mail software, and set up the option to not deliver the e-mail until 6:04 P.M. Not an exact number like 6 P.M. because that looks too obvious. Instead I would choose times that ended in 1, 2, 3, 4, 6, 7, 8, or 9.

Before I would leave at 5 P.M., I would make sure that the e-mail I was working on right until the end was sent out later on. Ideally, I wanted this e-mail to be sent to someone in a position of authority. Perhaps it was a question about a project I was working on, or maybe a "status update" (buzzword!), or just a quick note about an assignment I thought the boss man needed to be made aware of. It didn't have to be every day; in fact, you don't want this to happen every day—just enough for them to think, "Hey, this guy is sold out to our company—what an incredible work ethic!"

That could not be closer to the truth, either. You are dedicated, for Pete's sake. You start work every day at 5 A.M. while boss man over there is still probably reading his *Wall Street Journal* or more likely pressing the snooze button on his alarm clock.

Leave the Lights On

I know this section is going to make some people irate, and in particular, those who are "green sensitive." That is not who I am, so they'll just have to be tolerant of me and my indifference to their 'Do-It-My-Way-or-Else Platform."

Most companies have automatic lights that literally drove me bonkers. I could be working steadfastly at my computer, and those darn light sensors would shut my lights off because I was not active enough physically behind the computer desk. So I would have to raise my hand in the air or have some kind of muscle twitch to get those lights to turn back on. Sometimes, I just did not care, though, and worked in the dark, since all I really needed in the first place was the monitor I was working off of. It is imperative that you know whether you have automatic lights. If you do not, then always leave your light on. If work has commenced and you are late to the scene, the office lights being shut off will sell you out every time. So leave them on.

Beating the Light Sensors If the lights turn off automatically, there are a couple of tricks that can fix this for you so that they will never turn off again. First, take two paper clips and connect them with a 12-inch string. Take some scotch tape and tape it around one of the paper clips after you have attached it to the string. Then take one end of the string with the paper clip and slide it into a ceiling tile next to an air vent. What this will do is create movement on that string from the air coming out of the vent. The tape serves as a surface area for the air to blow against and get the string moving, allowing for the lights to always stay on (that is as scientific as I will get in this book). Other tricks include leaving a rotating fan running in the way of the light sensor, which will constantly leave the lights on as well.

Being Concise and Actionable with Your Research

I had about 10 different trading screens that I would run in the morning before I got to work, though since then, the number of screens I go through each day is a lot less (due to technology and efficiency), despite my being a full-time trader. I would wake up and get my morning dose of caffeine in the form of a soft drink. I would mosey over to my computer and starting looking through the charts.

Market Analysis

I would start with my trading plan first, by looking over the S&P 500 and SPY charts, which is still the index I use to this day for gauging market sentiment. This chart defined the direction I would trade. If we were in a strong bullish market, I would, of course, trade long and avoid the short positions altogether. If we were in a bearish market, I would stay net short with my positions, and often hedge myself for the dead-cat bounces that would eventually take place, and then ultimately reload and add new short positions once the market decided to move lower again.

The key to doing this and knowing which direction to trade in was becoming intimately familiar with my preferred index, which was the S&P 500. Some people track four or five indices and even dabble in foreign markets, and overlay them with multiple indicators and fancy oscillators. Do not do that unless there is a proven system you have unearthed that requires this. Just keep it simple. You can go to SharePlanner.com and see exactly how simple my trading plan is and how simple the charts are within that guide for the trading session ahead. I post it each day for free.

My main goal is to be concise and actionable. If I don't do that, why bother with the research? Now is not the time for a part-time trader to be philosophical about the economy or what he thinks the market should be doing. Instead, use this first morning task to determine what the index chart is telling you. Nothing more, nothing less. I recommend that you start off by becoming intimately familiar with just one index, whether you are a beginning or advanced trader. It is my opinion that if you study just one index up front, you'll find that is all you need to really track and gauge market sentiment.

Stay Clear of the Dow

The one index I would avoid making your primary chart is the Dow Jones Industrial Average. This is the index that everyone at the water cooler likes to report and talk about. But it is derived of the dollar movements of the actual stocks themselves. That means companies like 3M (MMM) have far more weight on the ups and downs of the Dow simply because it typically trades over $100 per share. It has almost four times as much influence as Microsoft (MSFT), which typically trades in the $20s. That means Microsoft would have to go up 4 percent in one day to have as much pull on the Dow as 3M's move of 1 percent, even though Microsoft is three times the market cap of 3M.

Knowing Your Trade Setups

I used to carry a notebook everywhere I went—to lunch, to the office, to meetings, and when I traveled. Most people did not know what that book was for, but it was small in nature, only 7.5-by-5, or just a shade bigger than a note card. Everything I did was for simplicity. Nothing was complex—how could I do it differently? I was a part-time trader. I would use only one page out of this book for each day of trading.

A typical page looked like the one in Figure 6.1, though it can look any way that you want it to be, to keep your trading simple and understandable to you.

Notice how simple I make it. I trust my analysis and know that if I write it down on the page, unless some unexpected new event transpires, I can trust my original thesis; therefore, I do not write the reasons for why I am trading the stock. That can be documented somewhere else, but not for the purposes of trading during the day. I am simply concerned with my entry, stop loss, target, and, of course, the stock that I am actually trading in.

Illegible to Others You can do this horizontally on a notecard if you want, but the main thing here is that I did not put a lot of sentences or descriptions on the text, because if I happened to make a mistake and leave it out in plain

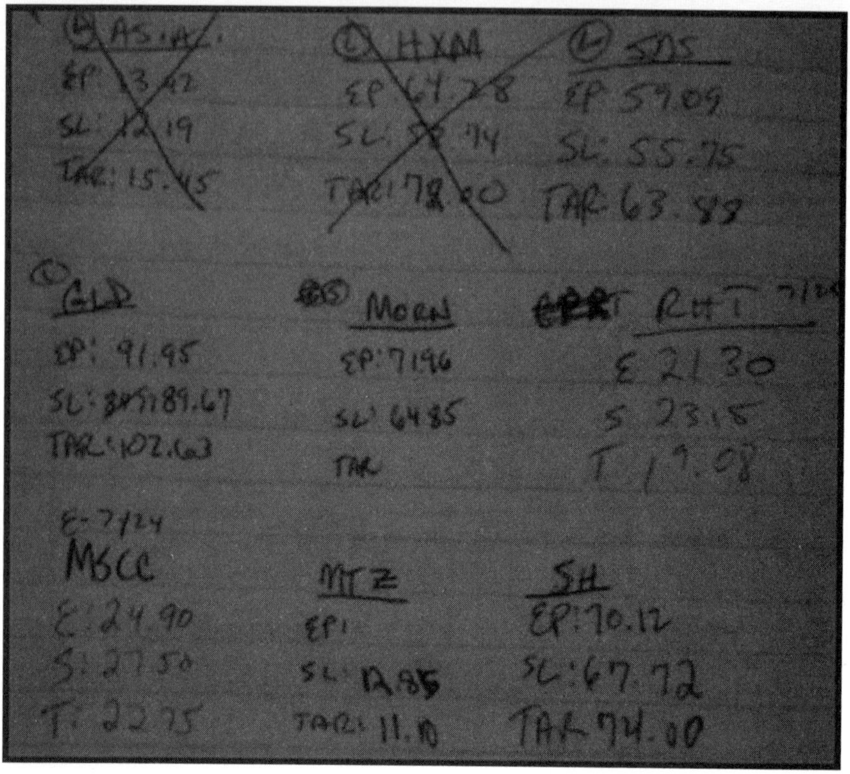

FIGURE 6.1 **My Notebook ofTrade Setups**

view for others to read—and I did that plenty of times by mistake—I did not want someone coming into my office without my knowledge and seeing everything that was on that piece of paper or note card, nor did I want them to know what it meant. Because I kept it understandable only to me, they would just assume that it was a part of my job and that they just did not understand its meaning.

Time-Zone Trading In order to be ready for when the market opens each day, you have to have your trading strategy and setups ready up front. If you are on Pacific Time, the market opens up at 6:30 A.M., which definitely has its advantages and disadvantages. First, unless you are a glutton for early mornings and little sleep, you will more than likely need to do your research at night, which would not be a problem for me, but some folks like to spend their evening winding down after a long, hard day—not taxing their brain until they go to sleep at night.

As I've said all along, though, you have to work your trading within the parameters of your job. However, one advantage to having the first couple of hours of trading at home is that you can, in the comfort of your home surroundings, get into your trade. When I would travel out West, I would always stay on East Coast time and wake up at 2 A.M. local time (which was really like waking up at 5 A.M. for me) and be able to trade the first few hours of each trading session before having to meet in the lobby with the rest of team I was traveling with. That is a huge advantage to have.

For me, though, living on the East Coast, I had to account for a 9:30 A.M. opening bell, but had the advantage of doing my research in the morning and being able to account for the activity in the European and Asian market as well as knowing what the futures did overnight.

Avoid the Clutter As a part-time trader, you do not have the luxury of being able to watch multiple markets, hundreds of stocks, intraday screening, and analysis. So do not prepare like one who can. Notice on the snapshot I provided from one of my days in Corporate America that I did not list 40 or 50 stocks. Instead, I have a handful of about 10 to 12 stocks. A number of those listed were carryovers from previous days of research where the setup did not trigger a buy or short action, but the trade setup was nonetheless still valid.

The last thing you want to be doing is going through pages of trade setups trying to find the ones that work for you. When you get to work, your trading should consist of acting on your morning's preparation. Have just a handful of stocks—no more than five to seven stocks that are your cream of the crop and worth taking action on. You can have others like I did, just in case price action warrants a trade in them, but keep your list of stocks that you follow to a minimum.

If you have too many trade setups that you are trying to act on, ask yourself what is the underlying, motivating factor for doing so. Often, it is out of a need to trade, and when that is the case, there is usually a horrible consequence that comes with it because when you are not going solely off of the top setups that you have, you will have fewer quality trade setups that you will be acting on, which means you are less likely to succeed consistently in the stock market.

Trade Your Plan

Avoid taking your list and modifying stop losses, targets, and, most important, the entry price once you are at work. If there is significant news released that day that is driving one of the stocks you are watching higher or lower and affecting your predetermined entry price, do not adjust that entry. Just scrap that setup and move on. It is far too difficult to be doing your job like you are supposed to while having to do secondary research on a given stock because of an outlier event affecting the trade setup you came to work with. As a full-time trader, you can do that. As a part-time trader—forget about it! Besides, that is why you have multiple setups on your watch list because if one does not work out, there are still five or six other setups that you can still take advantage of and profit off of.

Be methodical; follow your prework and premarket research that you woke up early to do. Trading on the job off of modified research is likely going to throw you into an emotional roller coaster, and the ultimate victim will be not only the capital you are trading with but your job as well. Like I said, keep it simple, and do not force the trade or follow some deep-seated need to trade. That means being willing to go through an entire set of days and not trading if that is what the market dictates.

Your Strategy for the Day Should Be Tailored around Your Workload

When I finally left the corporate desk to run SharePlanner.com and trade full-time, the transition was somewhat difficult for me, mainly because I felt that I could suddenly be more aware of my trading environment. You could say I got hyper about it. I had one screen that had a quadrant setup with the 1-minute, 5-minute, 30-minute, and the daily chart on the S&P 500. Because I could sit in front my monitors full-time without having to do some other job, I could watch 1-minute charts like they were going out of style.

I also tried to trade anything and everything that I saw. This was in direct contradiction to what had made me a successful swing trader for years on end. It was not that I thought I was suddenly becoming undisciplined in my trading—I just felt liberated to do so. In a way, that was detrimental to my trading success at first. I began trading far too often and incorporating far too many trading strategies to the point that I could not remember some of the positions I had on at times or the orders that were still active.

I bring this up because it is imperative that the manner in which you trade on a given day is tailored around your workload. If you are going to be loaded to the gills with meetings during the day, with very little downtime or the opportunity to simply be at your desk, then your focus should probably be on managing your existing positions and not adding to them. As we discussed earlier, smartphones are absolutely a requirement in today's technology-driven trading environment, and when you are going to have regular meetings throughout the time that the market is open, it is necessary to have a smartphone in hand or laptop access so that you can keep tabs on your position, and even more so if you decide to add a new position.

Remember, though—and this is important—to not trade regardless of consideration for what lies ahead in the day. Trading is serious business, and you do not want to approach it like a Las Vegas gambling addict who gets his thrills from pulling the lever. Do not be that trader. When your schedule does not give you a good opportunity to trade, do not force it—just step aside. It is the same concept as not forcing trades that do not have the right reward-to-risk setup. It is foolishness, and you need to avoid engaging in it.

Don't Go for the Easy Way Out

There are a lot of companies out there that offer services that seem too good to be true. My favorite is the Red Light–Green Light system. When you get the green light, you buy; when you get the red light, you sell; and if it is a yellow light, you just hold the stock if you are already in it. This kind of cheap-thrill trading is a bunch of nonsense. It does not work.

At some of the various trading conventions I attended in the past, I would find a number of different firms out there trying to woo people on the simplicity of their trading system and how it requires zero effort and zero maintenance or research. This is a fallacy in every sense of the word. I have met thousands of traders over the course of my career, and the one thing I can tell you with utmost certainty is that there hasn't been a single one that made it to where they are today because of some off-the-shelf "secret" trading program that tries to apply a set of variables to every stock for actively trading in a zero-risk environment. It just does not happen.

Avoid "Prop Firms"

Another word of caution for you: avoid the proprietary trading firms, better known as prop firms.

These "brokerages" are becoming highly popular and simultaneously blowing up accounts by offering users with account sizes under $25,000 a way to avoid pattern day-trading requirements by becoming a member of their prop firm and leveraging their account by insane levels like 10-to-1 and sometimes even more.

What is more disgusting is that many of these prop firms encourage you to pay them via credit card and then they provide the rest. But if you provide $2,500 in leverage, they will give you another $25,000 more in capital to trade with. But as soon as you lose that $2,500 dollars, that $25,000 goes away immediately.

The lunacy of these prop firms and what they promise is just another way to not offer a service but to also charge you a commission for every trade you make, as well as taking a percentage of your profits on the trades that you do make money off of (but never taking a share of the losses). They put the trader in a position to ultimately lose. They are leveraging your account, taking a cut from only those trades that profit, and then charge for each and every trade that you place. When your original capital runs dry, so does your relationship with them. Unless you deposit more money, they will simply kick you to the curb.

Most of these prop firms will take upward of 20 to 50 percent of your profits, but for the purposes of this discussion, let's say they take 20 percent. Over the course of the year, your winning trades amount to $200,000 in trading gains, while your losing trades amount to $180,000 in losses. They will take $40,000 out of the profits, and leave you essentially with a $20,000 loss on the year. That is insurmountable and unrecoverable if you are trading with a $50,000 account.

Ask yourself this: how many "self-made millionaires" have you ever met or heard of that started trading successfully through a prop firm? There are none because those who are looking to join a prop firm are skipping some of the most formative years of their trading education by taking a shortcut into the empty promises and doom of prop firm trading.

We covered a lot in this chapter, and it may be necessary to re-read this one a few times. No doubt about it, there are some funny anecdotes, but I cannot stress enough how important it is to prepare yourself for the trading day ahead each and every day before you get to work. After you arrive is not the time to do it. If you find yourself in that position, just skip trading for that day, and focus solely on the existing trades in your portfolio.

Your Best Friend Is the Person Who Works in IT

Much of what you can accomplish, what you can do, and the strategy you can employ as a trader will be centered around what your information technology (IT) department will let you do. For some companies this might be an entire department under Human Resources, and for others, it will be a stand-alone department.

Know How Your IT Department Works

The bigger the company, the more prominent this department will be. A small company will likely be run by only one or two people and be combined with Human Resources and some other similar departments. My experience in Corporate America wrapped it into Human Resources and a couple of other departments as well.

Along those same lines, the smaller the company, the less complicated and intricate the IT department is. Large companies have unbelievable amounts of resources dedicated to monitoring their systems, implementing software, and assuring that their servers remain up and running.

Regardless of the company size, it is very likely that the company has a system in place for monitoring their resources and how they are being used. You have to be careful about this. It is likely that you will never get down to the full extent of what kind of oversight that they employ on their resources.

This is why I am so passionate about being a solid employee. You do not have to save the world, just meet the expectations of the job before you as you try to trade your way out of workforce. Your job is your trading. If you do not maintain an acceptable performance level, your aspirations at a full-time career of trading will be cut short. You can rest assured that if you slack on the job, the full resources of the IT department will come down on you hard and lead to your immediate departure.

Small Companies

There are a lot of contrasts between large companies and small companies, and each carry their own pros and cons. Let's start with the small company. Here, you are likely to find a more family-oriented environment where you are expected to perform. How you do it is up to you, but you better perform because there is no way to hide like some are able to do in larger companies.

Harder to Blend In In small companies, you might be the only person in your department. Individual performance is key in small companies because the profits are often slim and the margins cannot be risked on a nonperforming employee. However, the resources that a small company will devote to the IT infrastructure will be only what is necessary. It is much less likely that they would have installed keystroke data, and servers will be likely hosted by a third party. Extensive oversight will be a little too much for a small company's budget when much of it can be observed with the naked eye and the capital can be applied to profit-generating activities.

In fact, making inroads with the boss man and others in small companies will help forge a strong bond between you and your coworkers. If you perform like you are supposed to, there is a good chance that they will not care that you trade and watch the financial markets. Some bosses may even let you have it as a perk to your job—like an incentive to doing a good job in your responsibilities. I am not saying this will be the case across the board; I am simply saying this scenario unfolds itself all the time and is not at all uncommon.

Just Do a Good Job Do your job well and they will probably leave you alone. If they do not, they probably have morons working at the helm who do not realize that a good employee with some outside interests is far better and much harder to replace than it is to bring on an unknown commodity, spend the time and resources to train him, and only hope that he is as good as the solid performer that was let go by the wayside. Give him that flexibility and he will do everything in his power to perform at such a level so that he does not lose the privilege he has become accustomed to. At least for me, that was the case when I was working for a smaller organization.

In the smaller company, they knew I had some outside interests in the financial markets, but they also knew I did not let it interfere with my daily activity. Besides, if you are a solid contributor to your organization, the company also realizes how difficult it is to compete with the larger companies in recruiting quality employees. And in my case, they definitely did not want to lay off me, Mr. High Performer, and replace me with an unknown, recent college grad and lose the experience that I had acquired and the time it took to acquire it. It just does not make sense, and such action by small companies does not happen much.

If they are going to fire you, they want to fire you because you suck at what you are supposed to be doing, and when they find out you have outside interests you have a greater passion for, they then have an explanation for why you are performing so poorly. Do not give them that reason.

Large Companies

With large companies, it is not so cut-and-dried. They see you, but you do not see them. At any moment they can be making a case against you for your immediate layoff. You just do not know—and that is regardless of whether you are an exemplary employee.

Too Big to Notice Initially Here is the caveat, though: these companies often employ thousands of employees, and with the size of the IT department they might have, they simply cannot dedicate the resources necessary to oversee all of the activities on an individual level. Instead, the IT department will more times than not rely on their tattletales on the ground. They wait for someone to come to Human Resources or IT to complain about a certain individual and the activities he or she is engaged in before they start to investigate.

Indiscriminate Toward Individual Performance When that happens, Human Resources will view you only as a number, not as the outstanding employee you may be known for being. If there is any substance to the complaint, they will more than likely follow up on you. To my knowledge, this never happened to me, but I have heard of it happening to others for things like streaming movies, music, running an online business and auctioning products off, and even online gambling.

Regardless of the reasons, it is not a good thing. If there is the slightest bit of personal activity being carried out on company resources and during company time, they are more than likely going to report this to your boss. Unless it revolves around pornography, illegal behavior, or compromising company secrets or private data, your activity will be forwarded to the boss man for him to determine the course of action to take against you, and he may or may not act on it. Once that happens, you will be parked in the boss man's office and asked a variety of uncomfortable question.

Going back to being the exemplary employee within your organization, in large companies, unless you give them a reason, it is doubtful anyone is going to file a complaint to have the boss man or IT start evaluating how you spend your minutes each day. In every instance I have seen, if you do your job and do it well and cover your tracks, no one is going to start heckling you about Internet usage or your time management.

Which One Is Better?

If I had to choose between a large and a small company, it would probably be a small one. You are not as inundated with rules, regulations, and red tape as is often the case in the larger organizations. Though the latter will often have far more resources at your disposal, I do not think it is enough to offset the frustrations that come with working for one. Quite honestly, there are far more variables to account for in a large corporate setting, which constantly left me in a state of paranoia for no reason at all when trading. But being conscientious as I am about nearly everything, it was easy to develop a mindset that anyone could sabotage my dreams of full-time trading.

While it is not advised, there is a much better chance of everything remaining status quo in regard to your relationship with the boss man if he becomes aware of your trading practices in a small company—that is, as long as your on-the-job performance is at least at par. In larger companies that employ thousands of individuals, it is really hit or miss when it comes to the repercussions for being exposed as a part-time trader. You are viewed only as a number in the system. If they determine that what you are doing should not be done, you have little in the way of bargaining chips that you will be able to use in your defense.

One Way to Turn the Tables My best advice is to develop a skill set that no one else has and to make yourself irreplaceable. Make it to where if they were to lay you off, the chances of the boss man's finding an equal would be slim to none. You do that, and it is likely that the boss man will vouch for you, and even let you continue trading without any repercussions. More so in the large companies than in the small ones, you are going to want to fly below the radar at all costs, and in Chapter 8, we go over this in much greater detail.

Ideally, Get to Know Someone from That Department

What really helped me in understanding IT and how it applied to my job function and flexibility was becoming friends with some of the people in the department. When I first started out in each of my jobs, I never knew any of the individuals, but whether it was a small or large company, I eventually knew a handful of folks from there.

You Only Need One

One such individual was named Greenwood. He was not a person that I would naturally be friends with because, for starters, he lived and breathed his job. The prospect of being noticed by the boss man, or better yet the boss man's boss man, would make him giddy as a schoolgirl. As you can imagine, these particular types aren't exactly the ones that I am aiming to make close friends of mine. They make me squeamish and cause me to bite my tongue more times than I would like when they start rambling on about which higher-up's secretary they got an e-mail from, or my personal favorite, who they happened to be on a foursome with during a recent golf outing. It is a creepy form of worship that is not deserved.

It really is not hard to befriend the folks in IT. Often (but not always, by any means), these people are geeky or considered "nerds" by society's standards. Trust me—there is nothing wrong with that, as I myself have plenty of nerdy tendencies that if fully known publicly in high school would have resulted in some atomic wedgies by the meatheads that roamed the hallways.

Do Not Be Turned Off by Their Standoffishness

On that same note, though, a lot of the folks in IT have personality complexes. They are extremely smart—in fact, they are usually brilliant. They flourished in college, in the advanced degrees that they achieved, and were a part of the computer clubs in high school. But they are often socially inept or used to being at the bottom of the social acceptance ladder. While they might be a bit standoffish at first glance, making friends with these individuals can come quite easy.

In the past, wanting to be acquainted with someone in the IT group was motivated by personal reasons, but I found that some of these people have made for some solid friendships over the years.

A Friendly Conversation Ensues

Back to the part that matters: finding a way into the IT world and its inner workings. Up front, you have to look at it from a tactical approach. I made friends with one such guy simply by noticing he was playing around with the latest Mac. I knocked on the door and started asking him questions. I was interested in what he had to say, which included question like:

"Hey, is that the newest Mac from Apple?"
"How did you get your hands on one of those?"
"What's the performance like?"
"Do you think it is better than any of the PCs on the market?"
"Is it customizable?"

After you have peppered him with these questions, and yes, often these questions will lead to longer responses than you might prefer, not to mention that most of the answers will not be entirely understandable due to the fact that they are probably talking 20 IQ points over your own. But here the conversation should segway into a more personal level of basic friendship:

"So where did you learn all this stuff? Did you study for it in college?
"What school did you attend?"
"No kidding, so did I."
"Hey, we should go grab a burger for lunch sometime."
"Awesome, I'll give you a ring the next time they unchain me from my desk."

You see there? After seven rather general questions, you have yourself a budding friendship in the making. Do not rush things, either; IT people, due to their high level of deductive reasoning, can become rather suspicious of your motives fairly quickly. An additional bonus is that if your wives hit it off, then you are rock-solid going forward. By the time you have notched a couple of lunches, you can probably start diving into the world of IT with him. Start with some general icebreakers like:

"So what is the IT department all about?
"What is it that you guys really do?"
"Does IT house their own servers or are they off-site?"

Start Digging In

Simple questions will make your newfound friend anxious to tell you more about what he does in the computer world. What is better is that often these conversations will evolve on their own into some more in-depth discussions that will reveal to you more details about what the purpose of the IT group is and its relationship with the employee and their activity on your work computers.

The previous questions can also lead to a hypothetical question such as:

> I was in another department speaking with someone about a project we were working on and I overheard this guy in the next cubicle over talking on the phone to someone who just bought this guy's homemade blueberry muffins online. That has nothing to do with his job, but he is using company resources to do it. How the heck does this guy get away with doing that?

His response will drive much of what you are able to do at your own workstation. If the response ends up sounding something like: "We monitor everyone's Internet activity, and if the user surpasses 25 percent of personal time on the Internet, he will be flagged and dismissed from his responsibilities." If you get a response like that, then you know that you have some actionable evidence about how to manage your time online in relationship to trading.

You may also be surprised by what he says if he responds with something like:

> We really do not monitor what people do. We'll check for spikes in bandwidth relative to other users or average usage in general, but unless we have suspicion we are not going to dive into the personal usage of an employee on the Internet. We just do not have the resources to do that.

If that is the case, you now know that as long as you keep your trading private and your performance on the job where you continue meeting expectations, you will be good to go.

What You May Find Out

There is a lot of technology out there for companies to utilize when it comes to anything and everything that you do on your computer. One of the more popular features is the keystroke function. There are plenty of software companies that provide this kind of technology, but essentially what this does is record every time you press a key on the keyboard.

For instance, have you ever had an e-mail that you wanted to fire off at the boss man that really showed how you felt about him and how he ran the operation? It felt good to type out the e-mail that insulted him in every known way. But, of course, you backspaced out the e-mail and removed all of the derogatory text. Guess what! That entire "wishful" e-mail was recorded in the company's keystroke archives, and if they ever needed to build a case against you for having you fired, that evidence would be there for the their use, even though you never saved anything or actually acted on what you really would have liked to say to him.

Workplace Armageddon

I remember one time sitting in my cubicle on the Wednesday before the Thanksgiving break. It could be somewhat of a ghost town in the office since everyone was just waiting around to get the long holiday weekend started. Essentially, everyone that came in that day would wait until after lunch and then see whether the coast was clear to sneak out without being noticed. It was a domino effect, with the starting piece being the boss man. Once he left, the people remaining would just start peeling off one by one. It was one of those unaccepted and unwritten rules that everyone denied doing but, when no one was looking, they all would engage in.

On one particular occasion I was sitting at my cubicle with my head on a swivel planning my getaway. The boss man had left, and of course he had some reason to be excited as well. He was on his way to being promoted to a vice president position in the company. Just as I was getting out of my chair ready to hit the road without being caught in the act, a friend of mine, who we called "Batman" for reasons unbeknownst to me (though he was quite the eccentric of character types), came running into my office gasping for air. He had just run full-throttle across the cubicle farm and into my little space.

He handed me a single sheet of paper—a printout of an e-mail he had typed up. It was about his immediate boss, the one who was about to be promoted to vice president. The letter was scathing, one of the boldest e-mails I had ever read. I swelled with pride for this man who embodied everything that I would have liked to say about this incompetent manager who was wreaking havoc on our careers with his inept ways of management. The best part was that he intended to send this to the company president that was looking to promote him.

From Noble to Idiotic My first response was very basic: "You definitely let him know how you feel about the promotion of Jim [our boss]."

The problem, though, was not in the subject or body of the e-mail, but the fact that he had actually sent the e-mail, by accident, to the person he was seeking to vilify. Yes, he was sending it to Jim.

This is where you enter crisis mode. I was going to do anything and everything I could for this man to keep him from being ruined from this one moment of horrible oversight. The good thing, as mentioned earlier, was that the boss man had already hit the town for Thanksgiving, so the chance he had read the e-mail, by our deduction, was slim to none. My first thought was to call Greenwood in IT and ask him to delete the e-mail. Unfortunately, he either was not going to touch that ticking time bomb or he was really telling me the truth when he said there was nothing that he could do about it.

Time for Plan B: The Boss Man's Office Now that I was willing to go to this extent, the whole thing was becoming a bit of an out-of-body experience. I felt like I was on a mission for the greater good. So we made our move inside the boss man's office. Once in there, though, we were immediately confronted with the cold reality of the computer appearing as if it had been shut down.

Our hope was that since he had only left 20 minutes earlier, the computer might still be accessible and that the monitor was only in power-down mode. Unfortunately, it was not. We were locked out. Username and password were required.

We were not done, though, because there was Plan C. (In hindsight, this probably should have actually have been Plan B). That was to simply recall the e-mail—a feature that is highly iffy when it comes to actually working. If the e-mail had been read, there was no way it would be recalled. First round of recall . . . nothing. Second try . . . nothing. Third attempt . . . nothing. For posterity's sake, we made a total of 10 recall attempts, all for nothing.

Losing Hope Maybe we were doing something wrong. So we tried it out on ourselves by sending and recalling an e-mail. We managed to successfully recall the e-mail when it had not been read but were met with failure when the e-mail was opened prior to the recall attempt.

The best (or, in the case of Batman, the worst) part of it all was that we discovered that each time you try to recall a message after it has already been read, it actually notifies the illegitimate recipient that you are trying to recall the message from them. That means an additional 10 e-mails were sent to this guy asking for the e-mail back!

To say the least, Batman probably had the longest Thanksgiving weekend of his life, but for all the wrong reasons. When Monday rolled around, he gingerly stepped back into the cube farm, waiting for his fate. When Jim called him into his office, the infamous and awkward stare-down between boss man and employee took place, with the former rocking back in forth in his plush leather chair.

"You're an idiot!"

"Excuse me?" replied Batman.

"Seriously . . . how could you be that big of an idiot? How? You sent me the e-mail! What were you thinking?!"

And Batman's time employed ended with a subtle but honest reply: "At least you know how I feel now."

Caution at Every Corner

The point of this all is to realize that you have to be very, very cautious about the technology that you are using. You might not ever be confronted with the kind of problem I have just talked about. However, it is a microcosm of the slipups you can have with technology. I had many of them, and much of what I talk about in this book comes from my own mistakes as a worker and part-time trader.

What you always have to do is err on the side of caution. Do not do anything that will get you noticed or figured out. You are trying to trade, not cure the ills of Corporate America (and just for clarification, capitalism is by far the best kind of economic system you can have). Do not cloud your objective by setting yourself as some Don Quixote. You mission is to stay at your current job long enough, whether it be months or years, so that you can transition successfully from the world of part-time trading to that of the full-time trader.

■ Understanding Their Policies and Designing Your Trading Around Them

Once you get familiar with the corporate policies toward Internet usage and after you know firsthand from those inside the IT organization how they operate, it will be necessary to modify your trading strategy as necessary.

Consider reading the corporate manual. Yes, that blasted booklet that outlines the impersonal nature of corporate policies. There is a 99.9 percent chance that there will be a whole section carved out and dedicated to Internet usage and how you may use your computer in such a way that does not lead to your immediate dismissal.

Working Your Way Around Obstacles

Here's the thing—if your corporate policies state that they have a zero-tolerance policy for personal Internet use that will lead to an immediate reprimand or firing, then that is probably a good indication that you should avoid using the Internet for trading, and instead rely more heavily on handheld technology like smartphones and tablets. Just make sure that if you use a tablet, you are not connecting to the company's Wi-Fi. Instead, you will want to make sure that you have a cellular plan dedicated to accessing the Internet. With speeds like 4G LTE that most companies now offer, the mobile experience of using cell towers is very comparable to many Wi-Fi networks.

When a company says they "reserve the right to do so" in their policies, it usually means "Do not give us a reason to monitor your every move." Therefore, you probably have more flexibility when it comes to accessing your online brokerage than what they want you to believe.

Saving Tips

Another quick tidbit that most people do not even realize they are doing sometimes but nonetheless they expose themselves to: it can be quite risky when saving files or installing programs to the company network's servers. Typically, there are two places that you can save documents to: the first is your hard drive on your computer. The second is the server space that companies give each employee to save their files to. Most companies want you to save your files to the space allocated to you on their servers because they are usually backed up, if not daily, at least weekly, and in case you leave the company on bad terms, they do not lose any files you might have tried to delete prior to your exit.

To say the least, I was against having any of my personal stuff (and I tried to limit anything personal) on the server, because once they made it through one backup cycle, they were there for all eternity. You do not get it back, and it is there for the boss man's taking should he want it. You could say I suffered from paranoia, but I also realized it was that paranoia that kept me from doing something incredibly stupid (not really, but I at least thought so). I was paranoid to such an extent that I figured they had some software I wasn't aware of that probably backed up the files on my computer as well. As a result, each night when I left the office, if I left my computer (when I had a laptop) in the office, I would unplug the network cable that connected to my computer to prevent any remote access to my computer.

Search Out the Guest Connection

Also, because I kept my working files on my computer (I would upload them to the server only if I had to or if I was required to for others to use), I would access the guest connection and not the internal network that required you to log on with password and username.

Most companies will have a protected network access and a guest access that does not require you to log on with your "identifying credentials." This is great because if you do not have to log on, you will not be tracked outside of that pesky IP address, but it is much more difficult to prove the user behind the computer by matching IP addresses, particularly since you did not use a username and password to access the internet.

Keeping Your Phone to Yourself

To add to the Internet usage aspect, do not—and I mean do not—access your company's Wi-Fi through your smartphone or tablet. Once you do that, any activity you on your own smartphone is deemed the same as doing it on your company-issued workstation.

I used to always have people trying to find out what my cell phone number was so that if I was not in my office, away at a meeting, in another office, or at the beach playing on a "sick day," they would be able to reach me. Let's just say, if they call you when you are at the latter, it is hard to cover up your whereabouts when they can hear the seagulls squawking in the background.

Don't Call Me Maybe I was on vacation once (literally), and on the slopes of some of Salt Lake City's finest mountain peaks getting ready to go down some of the best courses the world has to offer. Right before I began the descent down, my cell phone rang. I did not know who it was, but out of curiosity I answered it anyway.

"Ryan Mallory! This is Edward. Listen, you wouldn't mind taking a moment to explain to me about the competitive consumer price analysis you did on that contract you finalized right before leaving for vacation, would you?"

CLICK!

Another phone call later on . . .

"Hey, Ryan, Edward again. Listen, I know you are on vacation, but if I can just have 135 minutes of your time to explain exactly what went down during your negotiation session, I'd appreciate it."

To say the least, I never gave out my phone number ever again. Good ole' Edward managed to get it from the secretary that promised to guard it with her very life and to not make it available unless I was in a state of cardiac arrest on the floor (even then, I wanted her to wait a few minutes before she made it available to anyone, just in case I snapped out of it).

After that vacation, I came back with a changed phone number. People who tried to call me tried relentlessly to access me at that number. The problem was that I was paying for that phone with the minutes the corporation was consuming on a daily basis. When the secretary asked me to update her on my new phone number, I gave her one that was a single digit off. It was none of her business. I came to work, and if they wanted to contact me, they could do so through more traditional means, like waiting for me to be back at the landline at my desk.

Trying to Buy Me Off It got even better, though, because the Edwards, Debbies, and Garys grew frustrated with their inability to access me when I was away. Ultimately, they got me a cell phone. They asked me to permanently transfer my personal phone number to them and use their corporate "Obama-Phone" for personal and company matters.

Tempting to have a free cell phone—but no!

So I carried two phones around going forward, but then that also came to a quick end when I started getting phone calls late at night, asking me to bail out the boss man and come back into work for an evening shift. I acquiesced once, but only once. After that, the cell phone was left on my desk at work, and essentially it stayed there unless I was on travel. You see, if you want me to be on call, you should have put that in my contract when I signed up. If they wanted me to be on call around the clock, they would have to realize they better start paying me to be someone who was on call around the clock.

Installing Company Apps

I have started seeing where companies are coming out with their own smartphone and tablet apps for employees to use in conjunction with their job. Often, it is some tailored application providing them with easy access to the company intranet. I suspect as applications in general continue to grow in popularity, so will the need for companies to create them for their employees to use and have them "wired in" around the clock. However, by installing them on your personal phone, you are giving them a foothold into your personal life at no additional cost to them.

I've actually spoken with IT personnel at companies that offer these applications for employees, and they will not install them on their own personal smartphones because of privacy concerns that they determine to be too intrusive. The same logic that goes into not syncing your phone with company Wi-Fi should also be applied with the smartphone apps. You are simply surrendering your privacy when you install these applications on your own personal devices. If they want you to have it bad enough, they will pay for you to have that company smartphone or tablet.

Some Final Thoughts

By now you understand the important role the IT department plays in your ability to trade successful as a part-timer at a full-time job. Every company has a different policy and approach to how they monitor Internet and workstation usage. However, there will no doubt be some common threads among all of them. Unfortunately, some will be extremely strict and overbearing with their zero-tolerance policies. When that is the case, you will have to rely more heavily on handheld devices and personal tools, as well as a more restrictive trading strategy.

Most companies have a more moderate approach to how they track you and your network usage, and it will most likely be on an as-needed basis. If you are not bringing attention to yourself for all the wrong reasons, it is probably okay to say that you will not be given much flak about your need to trade in the stock market and polish your part-time trading skills in the process. Just make sure to play it safe, and err on the side of caution to make sure you are irreplaceable and doing all that is expected of you on the job.

Small companies will likely be easier to navigate, but because of the tighter-knit environment among coworkers, it will be much harder to remain ho-hum about your trading passion.

Flying Below the Radar

Much of what this book revolves around is not becoming a distraction in the workplace and having others become suspicious of your daily activities as a part-time trader. Like the old adage of "minding your own business," you truly have to do this as a part-time trader. First, you do not have time to partake in squabbles. I realized this early on, as my main objective was to eventually leave the company and become a full-time trader. Getting involved in office politics would only derail my mission.

Do Not Become a Distraction

When the boss man wanted me to do an assignment that I thought did not add value to the company, instead of starting some kind of e-mail war or dysfunction within the organization, I just went with it. I did not want to willingly create enemies because, in doing so, I would have a person who was determined to see my demise in the company. As a part-time trader, I was not going to let somebody I disagreed with try and find some dirt on me, exaggerate it (i.e., complain that I do not work but just trade stocks all day) and thereby wreck my dreams and ambitions, only because I originally felt the need to settle a score with him over a petty disagreement about company objectives.

It is important to guard yourself and your privacy. You could literally spend just one minute a day trading on the job, but if they knew you did that and were doing well at it, the assumptions would spiral out of control. Before long, you would be sitting in the boss man's office explaining how you were still a "company man" dedicated to the long-term vision of the corporation.

So do not share anything with anyone about your trading. Absolutely nothing. You have nothing to gain and everything to lose in doing so.

■ Do Not Be a Clicker

Speaking to the idea of not raising suspicion is when someone walks into your office and the first thing they hear is the immediate sound of the mouse click. Do not kid yourself, either; usually, it is a ton of clicks that must take place, and if they walk around your desk to get in plain view of what is on your monitor screen, you find yourself ferociously scrambling to get that tiny little pointer on the upper right hand screen over that tiny little "X" that will allow you to close out the window.

It is kind of like the horror movies that have some axe murderer chasing some unsuspecting woman down the street, and once she gets to her car, she frantically tries to find the key to unlock the door. After she loses valuable time doing this, she then has to get the key in the keyhole. After scraping 90 percent of the car paint around the keyhole off, she finally gets the door unlocked and ajar. At this point she is in the seat, and she is really in trouble if there is a different ignition key than the one she used to unlock the door, but once she does get that key in the ignition, the car just turns over repeatedly, over and over again, and she winds up being another victim on the axe murderer's killing spree.

Your fellow coworkers are like that axe murderer. Once you start panicking and trying to minimize the screens or simply closing them out because they showed up in your office unannounced, they become interested in what is on that monitor that is only for your eyes. They will stroll over casually like that is not what they are coming over there to do. But rest assured, they have only one objective in mind and that is to know what is on your screen.

The boss man is the absolute worst about this. If he hears that mouse start clicking (and like I said, it never takes just one click like it should), he might as well fire up the chainsaw because he is going to chase down a visual of that monitor no matter how bloody it has to get.

The Mouse Click Alternative

Save yourself the time and anxiety of worrying about their seeing what is on your screen. Let's say you have just placed a trade and you are taking a few minutes to observe the price action, and then in walks the boss man.

Do not panic. Better yet, do not look up. Use your peripheral vision to know that he is there, but do not look up. First of all, you will look intense like you are absorbed in your job and you just cannot break it off. You are wired in, and that is what the boss man likes to see. Stay expressionless as well; do not change your expression because if you show any fear, worry, or anxiety about his walking in, the start cord is going to get pulled on that bone-crushing chainsaw instantly.

The next step is key, and it may take some practice. Some of you may already use it, and that is fantastic. Whenever you are on the computer, you always have at least your left hand on the keyboard, or when you are typing you have both, obviously. When the boss man walks in, you take your thumb and push down and hold the "ALT" key. Then, with the ring finger, you strike the "TAB" key but without letting go of the "ALT" key. You will have a box pop up front and center on your screen and you simply "TAB" your way to the programs until you find the screen you want to replace your current display with.

If you have no other programs running, you are screwed because that window is not going away, without clicking the mouse. So always make sure you have at least two windows up and available on your screen at the same time. If you do not, you are then doing the equivalent of dropping the keys on the ground with the crazy man nipping at your heels. It sends sheer panic through the body when you have no other windows to "ALT+TAB" on and you will have to resort to a last-second attempt to close out the window without being exposed.

Lowering the Bar

Let's assume that you are able to avoid the pitfalls that come with minimizing or exiting out of whatever trading screen you might be in. But there is this annoying little taskbar found at the bottom of your window. You have to get rid of this. The taskbar tells them exactly what programs you are running, what applications you have minimized, and anything else you might be wanting to keep on the downlow.

There is good news, though—you can have this taskbar minimized at all times unless you hover your mouse over it down below. It is extremely easy to set this up. Using a Windows-based computer, you simply right-click anywhere on the taskbar and select "Properties." Once the dialog box pops up, click on the check box that reads "Auto-hide the taskbar" and then the "OK" button down at the bottom.

Mission accomplished!

Workplace Peeping-Toms

Maintaining monitor privacy cannot be overstated. The two tricks of the trade I just described will go a long way in doing just that. However, one of the biggest mistakes you can make when it comes to privacy from co-workers is keeping your computer unlocked when you get up and walk away from your workstation.

Squatter's Rights I remember one such occasion where I went to the soda machine probably 20 paces from my work desk. As I was contemplating my third soda choice of the day to help keep me awake on the job, one of those overwhelming, dastardly Debbies walked into my office and assumed the controls of my workstation.

When I walked back into my office, to my astonishment, she told me that IT was updating some piece of software on her workstation and that she was just using mine for the time being. E-mail, trading portal, and a few charts had been minimized, but they were still there from hours earlier; I just had not yet closed them out.

The problem facing me was that she was one of those people that you could not just simply ask get out of your chair because she would not likely get up. She would see it as some kind of challenge. Of course, I did not want to raise suspicion that I was trying to hide something from the company because I was just trying to keep my privacy in check from her. Eventually, I just made up some hokey excuse that I needed to access my e-mail to find out where the next meeting was because I was late. She offered to get it for me. I refused to let her do that and made it sound like getting to this meeting was a life-and-death matter.

Phew! Crisis averted.

But I could have easily avoided this from ever happening in the first place had I just hit the "CONTROL+ALT+DELETE" keys to keep anyone from accessing my account by locking my computer while I was away. This whole event unraveled shortly before I gave my two-week notice, and to this day I do not know what she learned of my part-time trading, if anything. The problem was that I had been compromised, and had I not left when I did, perhaps things might have become much more difficult for me.

■ Avoid Telling Anyone that You Are a Trader

With the advent of social media, our private lives are exposed for the world to see—sometimes willingly, and unfortunately, at times, it is shown to the world unwillingly. A word of advice for you as a part-time trader: Do not talk about it on Facebook, LinkedIn, Twitter, or any other forum that a co-worker might have access to.

When I was still laboring away in the corporate world, I never, ever accepted a friend request from a friend or colleague at work. If I mentioned something about trading, and I made sure I never did, I did not want that status update flashing on their news feed at home. If you are going to put something on Facebook about trading (and this can go for nontrading topics as well), expect that the world will see it, even if you have the strictest of privacy settings. When it comes to social media, you can count on the fact that there is never going to be a true sense of privacy in regard to what you post.

So stay away from posts that would reveal more about your life and in particular your trading. If you would not be comfortable with every person in your workplace knowing about it, do not post about it.

More Importantly, Do Not Involve Others

Early in my corporate career, there was a guy who was interested in following my trades. He was a good friend of mine, so I had no problem in sharing those "picks" with him on a near-daily basis. However, this guy could not handle the stress of trading. He did nothing outside of the trading opportunities that I would provide him with, in terms of making himself a better trader. Instead, he would call me each morning and ask, "So what are we trading today?" I typically would reply with some of the stocks on my radar and the entry prices I was pursuing. I am quite certain he would jump into any pick that I gave him.

Low-Beta Stress On one such occasion, the stock was Microsoft at $25.20. He placed a limit order like I had told him to do in the past, and he got filled at the same price I did. Fifteen minutes later, I received a panicky phone call in which the first words out of his mouth were, "IT'S TANKING! IT'S TANKING!" At this point, my stomach was in my throat. I popped up my brokerage screen to find Microsoft trading at $25.18. That's right, it had tanked a whole two pennies. When I questioned his fears, his response was, "It just doesn't look good, man. We gotta get out . . . NOW!" At this moment he made a noise that was essentially an inverted "hissing" sound, followed by three pounding sounds of his fist against the desk.

Looking back at this, the story was comical. The guy had no business trading stocks and probably should relegate his trading to long-term interest-bearing assets. Believing that Microsoft was tanking simply because it was two cents lower than my entry price was ludicrous.

I got to thinking after this particular experience, wondering why in the world this guy was acting so crazy about such a small pullback (if you want to call it that). What would a normal loss be like to this guy, say, of 4 or 5 percent? Would he go postal on the whole place? Probably not, but what if in the future he got into a biopharmaceutical company on my recommendation, and it tanked 8 or 9 percent on a bad piece of news unexpectedly. While that rarely happens to me in my trading, it is at least worth exploring the what if's and his reaction to such a scenario.

I concluded that this guy was a huge risk. If he had a particularly bad trade happen, and it was my recommendation that got him into it, there is a good chance it would create some bad blood between the two of us, and as a result he would probably want some revenge for his losses. There is no better way of doing this than by simply shooting off an e-mail to Human Resources informing them of my trading and really making it look like it was something horribly wrong that I was engaged in. The mere thought of that really bothered me. I realized that we would probably be friends as long as he continued to profit off of me, but the moment that he lost some money that meant something to him, all hell would break lose, and I could be the biggest loser after HR straightened out the situation.

No Stocks for You! As a result, I withdrew from providing him with any more trading opportunities. He would follow me into any trade that I would take but rarely follow me out of a trade. This is one horrible trait to have, when you cannot sell a stock that you know you should be selling, simply because the gains are not enough for you, you cannot accept a loss, or your expectations are far too high for the trade.

Could you imagine the pressure I would've been under to keep everybody in the office happy had I let all of them into my trades? One larger-than-average loser and I would probably have to get armed escorts to get me out of the building.

The takeaway here is to keep your trades to yourself. There is nothing more problematic than letting folks know about your trading habits because as soon as they know about it, they are going to want in on them. You see, for everyone who is not a trader, it does not dawn on them to consider measuring the risk and reward associated with the individual trades, nor can you as a trader understand their mindsets when it comes to the emotions of greed and fear and how they will handle a losing trade. Instead, for your coworkers, it is those three or four letters that they desperately seek to make a lot of money off of. To them it is all about the stock pick. If there is money to be made, you can rest assured that your coworkers are going to want in on it.

What is worse, though, is that you will have to babysit every one of these people who are trading your stock recommendations. They will constantly be coming into your office to ask about the current state of the trade:

"Where's it going?"
"How high do you think it will go?"
"Where do you want to get out?"
"Do you not think it could go higher?"

This is all they will care about and all that they will ask you about.

Early in my corporate career, I had over a dozen people coming into my office to ask about my trades. I felt like some kind of bookie running an illegal gambling ring (though, of course, I was not).

To say the least, I could not be the solid employee that I knew I had to be because I had all these people coming into my office asking for more trades and what they should do with the existing ones, and telling me how much money they hoped to make off of them. But these people could not contain themselves; they would, of course, have to tell these friends about this great new gig they had going on with Ryan down the hallway. So then, of course, I would have to come up with some creative approach to get rid of each and every one of these poor souls just hoping to make an extra buck.

It is a lose-lose situation to try and involve others in your trading. You are not running a charity here, and if ever there is a day where it all hits the fan, you will be thrown under the bus faster than you could imagine.

Keep Things Business as Usual

There were countless times in the office where a huge sell-off in the markets spurred on "Did you see the Dow Today?" discussions. This usually arose when the Dow was down 200 points or more. No one paid attention to the S&P or Nasdaq. The S&P 500 could be down 30 points and the Nasdaq down 50 points, and no one would notice if the Dow did not tank with them.

On one such occasion, I remember a woman stating that exact panic question about the Dow's sell-off. Of course, I saw it, but could I tell her that? No way! What would have been a real kicker is if I had told her, "Yeah, I saw that—good thing I liquidated my long positions and took on a 3× Ultra

Bear Financial ETF (though I hate leveraged exchange-traded funds [ETFs]) and made a boatload of cash off of your misery for limiting yourself to the world of long-only IRAs."

When everyone is losing their hide in their 401(k), the last thing you want to be doing is fist pumping with excitement over capitalizing on the new market downtrend. That will evoke jealousy and bitterness toward you, which will ultimately lead to a bounty being placed on your head.

Mild Man Trader

I would play the fool. Completely oblivious to what the stock market was when asked. If questioned, "Did you see the Dow sell off?" I would reply with, "What store is running that sale?" I simply played oblivious to what they were saying. Sure, there were times when the markets were hitting extremes in their cycle that I would see these individuals sell at the bottom, or during periods of market exuberance, where they finally decided to jump back in at the top of a market, that I would have liked to help them out otherwise, but I simply could not do it. Like Clark Kent, I had to keep secret my true identity.

The Contrarian Indicator

Let me tell you, though, coworkers make for some of the best market indicators. They represent a factor that moving average convergence/divergence (MACD), stochastics, and other indicators cannot capture, and that is fear and greed. Since having become a full-time trader, I really miss having access to that indicator. I was able to make a lot of profits off of my coworkers without their ever knowing it.

I even had a name for this unbelievable tool: The Larry Indicator. That's right, named after the namesake of the beleaguered Larry employee as well. You see, good ole' Larry was a company man and would remain a company man his entire life. He had been there for 35 years and was nice as can be. He walked around with the pocket protector in his right breast pocket, and would bring in the local newspaper each and every day. He would read that newspaper from front to back. The man was practically untouchable at what he did.

I would go in there each day to read the sports section while he read the front page and business sections. While I enjoyed reading my sports on traditional print, I also enjoyed listening to his comments about the markets as the indices trended up and down and up again.

He knew what some AP writer wrote in generic terms about the previous day's market action. When conditions got bad, he wore it all over his face. He would make comments like "I have to retire, I cannot keep letting everything I worked for all these years get swallowed up by the market," or sometimes I would yell across the hallway on a very bad day in the markets and after a more extended pullback, "Larry, that Dow thing you are always are talking about, its down like 225 points right now!" When his emotions reached DEFCON 1, he would reply with, "Do not tell me anything more about it; I have put it all back into a money market account!"

Buy, Buy, Buy! At that point, I knew I had my buy signal. I would start buying stocks and bullish ETFs very aggressively. I honestly do not think I ever lost off of that indicator. Not once! I would like to have him be a consultant to my own trading now, but if he understood why I wanted him around, I think his market magic would quickly disappear.

I had some others that I had marked for my bearish indicators. I had the "Dopey Darlene" Indicator, the Jovial Jolene Reversal, and many others. Their emotions of fear and greed could almost be plotted on a chart. They were unbelievable and timely.

Funny Stories with a Serious Undertone

While these might be humorous stories, the premises behind them are of utmost seriousness. You are at work to get your job done, and in such a way you can simultaneously pursue your career as a full-time trader through the purview of a part-time trader on the job.

Far too often when someone pursues a trading career, it is not about the simplistic reasons of providing a livelihood for themselves. Instead, there is this empty void in their lives that they feel the need to fill. Whether it is due to some problematic childhood, or through the need to pad a lack of self-esteem with a feel-like-a-winner mentality, or some other hidden motive, none of them will help you succeed and more times than not will lead to the implosion of your capital.

Now, Most Importantly The main objective in trading is to trade in a manner that offers an acceptable probability to profit at an acceptable level of risk. If you are not running every trade you make through this lens, you are at risk to never make it into the world of full-time trading.

Most people in the workplace have never even heard of the concept of selling short a stock. Once you have a few winning trades under your belt or even more, a full year or two of successful trading, therein lies the need to boast, to brag, and to tell others about it. Most men who get into trading do so out of the desire to win. Of course, they want to make money and lots of it, but psychologically they want to win as well. That is a dangerous mindset to have because being good at losing is just as important as being good at winning.

If you cannot systematically lose, when the trade has shown you that it is a losing proposition, then you should not trade at all. Most traders have a hard time booking a losing trade.

It is not that I want to have losing trades, but it is the realization that there will be plenty of losing trades no matter how successful I am at trading. Far too often, though, traders will double-, triple-, and even quadruple-down losing trades out of desperation to be a winner. I have literally seen people unwilling to take a losing trade of 3 percent but will risk a whole year of gains just to save face in hopes of coming out a winner. It sounds like lunacy, I know, but there are plenty of traders who easily fall into this trap each and every day.

Winning is not your objective. Having a winning trade is not your objective, either. Profiting over the course of a period of time by which you judge your performance is your goal, your mantra, your purpose. Your ego, self-esteem, and desire to feel like a winner personally and in front of others cannot be a part of your game plan.

Do Not Spike the Ball

Too many professional athletes are "divas" within their profession. They are high-maintenance individuals who need the praise and applause of their fans and peers. As a young boy growing up, I had the privilege of watching Barry Sanders play each Sunday afternoon. What stuck out about him to me and what I learned from him in my trading was how to approach the game, and in my case, my profession. When Barry Sanders scored a touchdown, he did not do some self-celebratory end-zone dance. Instead, when he scored, he took the football and handed it to the ref and went back to the sidelines. He acted like he had been there before, like it was expected and routine.

Today, there are traders who spike the football on social media, on the financial news networks, and in interviews about how great a trader they are. They are metaphorically spiking the football and revealing the amateur state of their trading. When you trade and when you profit, act like you have done it before and move on to the next trade. Look for the next trade you can attempt to profit on. Do not relish the trade or tweet about it, and as a part-time trader in the corporate world, you must never gloat about it in the office. When you do not follow this advice, your objective in trading becomes more about your image, and you start trading in such a way that will preserve your image and nothing else.

Know your purpose in your trading and what you are setting out to achieve, and trade accordingly.

Adding a Passive Income to Your Day Job

When you are a part-time trader, by its very definition, it means that you have a better source of income available than what you are reaping from the markets. If that was not the case, then you would more than likely opt to be a full-time trader. When I left my job, it was because the opportunity that existed as an employee paled in comparison to the benefits of transitioning into a full-time trader. But up until that very moment I quit my job, the benefits suggested that I should remain with my current employer. Trust me, if I could have left one minute earlier, I would have.

It's a Supplement—Not the Main Source

The benefit of becoming a successful part-time trader is that you still get to do that and your day-job. If you are one of the few who actually enjoy their job environment, and long-term your employer is fine with your trading, then you have a scenario to be extremely envious of. Not only do you have your job that you really like, which makes me assume that they are paying you well, too, but you also get to supplant that paycheck with your trading activities. In essence, you can make a very nice and comfortable life for yourself.

Combining the Day Job with Part-Time Trading

For most of us, though, our trading and desire to ultimately become that full-time trader, far outweigh the long-term benefits of our Monday-through-Friday job. As a result it is easy to lose sight of the difference between the supplement income and the main course. The losses as a part-time trader do not seem as painful as they do when you are trading full-time. The main reason for it is that you know if you go through a string of bad trades, you are only affecting the capital that you are trading with. In fact, you can pay back those losses by dipping into your paycheck to recoup them, even though that is not the backdrop you should have to your trading.

Overall, the income that you make from your job still supports you and your family without a hiccup. Therefore, it is easy to not take losses seriously and that can be a huge problem. Feeling the pain of trading losses, seeing what you did wrong, and avoiding making the same types of mistakes again in the future is hard to notice when those losses can so easily be offset.

On the flip side, for the full-time trader, the capital you enter full-time trading with is the capital you will be stuck with. You will have to provide yourself with a stream of income from it to support you and your family, as well as steadily grow the portfolio year after year. To say the least, trying to pull that off can be very difficult and is often the reason for why most traders simply do not make it in this profession. That is why trading part-time while having the full-time job to take care of all the bills and day-to-day activities is an incredible asset to have, because then with your portfolio you can grow as a trader without all the pressures of trying to do it on your own full-time and support yourself and family with the income or lack of income generated from your trading.

Become Systematic in Your Trading

In general, people tend to make their trading far too complicated and difficult, which along with many other reasons that I've already discussed leads to hard-to-grasp success that most traders are desperate for. Trading needs to feel natural and systematic. You need to understand what you trade and why trade for a reason.

Trading Should Be Natural to You

In my own trading, I do not take trades for simply taking them. I do not trade stocks out of boredom, out of need, or out of desire for some type of excitement. I trade stocks to extract a consistent stream of profit out of the market. I trade stocks within a defined price range; there are certain stocks that I simply know up front I will not trade. For instance, I am not trading real estate investment trusts (REITs). I also shy away from insurance companies. Penny stocks—no way! If the stock is trading below $3, the company better have an incredible reward-to-risk ratio, and a price pattern that leaves little to the imagination.

The "Main Thing" I am obsessed in trading and life in general with "keeping the main thing the main thing." And the *main thing* in my trading revolves around this one all-encompassing statement to my trading: does this trade represent an acceptable probability to profit at an acceptable risk?

All my trades must go through this litmus test. If the stock has a great price pattern but a level of risk that I cannot afford to take, then forget about it. I will not place the trade, no matter how promising the odds are of profiting are. Likewise, if I find a trade with an ideal level of risk, and for me that is usually in the range of 2 to 4 percent of my overall position value, but a trade setup that has less than the desirable level of possible success attached to it, I will simply move on to the next potential trade. That means if the price pattern looks good, but if there is a heavy level of resistance, where historically the price has struggled to break through, I am going to assume that if tested again, the odds are the price action will fail to break through, and I will ultimately lose on the trade.

That's Who I Am

I am primarily a swing trader who only dabbles in day trading, or when a solid opportunity presents itself. Here are some other facts about my trading that I have defined and do not leave to interpretation one bit. How I trade is reflected in these statements and these statements in my trading.

As a trader, I focus on equities and try not to dabble in exchange-traded funds (ETFs) and other trading vehicles.

Chart Types I trade primarily off of daily charts and secondarily off of five-minute and weekly charts. The daily charts are my source for spotting price patterns, defining risk, and ideal volume patterns. I use candles on all my charts for defining price movements within a period.

The five-minute charts help me for staging my entry into a stock. If the price is overly extended on the intraday chart, I am going to hold off on trading the stock, until it has come back down to earth some. Nine times out of ten, I reap the benefits of not trading on an overextended chart in the five-minute time frame. Weekly charts help me for spotting long-term support and resistance levels that might not have been seen looking at eight months of daily price action on the daily chart. Also, weekly charts tend to be a little bit smoother, and lacking the crazy gap ups and downs and candle shadows, that tend to dirty up a daily chart.

Trend Following the Markets While I willingly trade both to the long side and short side, and often at the same time among different stocks, I will ultimately allow for my trading direction to be dictated by the market's bullishness or lack thereof. I do not try to front-run market reversals, or allow my opinion on economic fundamentals taint my view on the technical analysis of the charts, the S&P 500, and other indices that I follow. To say the least, I am not a contrarian in my trading. I take what the market is willing to give me. I leave my beliefs and opinions out of the equation, and simply trade what I see and not what I think. Because I do this, I am able to minimize those pesky emotions of greed and fear that try to overcome all of us in some form or another.

That means at times, I am taking trades that I really hate taking. That is what being systematic is all about. I have had some of my best gains come from stocks that set up perfectly and looked great in every time frame and from every angle. The problem was that I had a horrible bias against the company. I have been that way with a handful of industries in the past. Ironically, my best gains are usually from these types of trades (minus the REITs and insurance companies, of course), often because I am being dragged into the trade kicking and screaming because the trade setup is so perfect.

On the flip side, those stocks that I tend to have a positive predisposition toward are usually the ones I lose on, because my view of them is tainted, so when I am looking at stocks and a particular company pops up that I have warm and fuzzy feelings for, I am falling victim to confirmation bias, rather than rationally looking at a stock that might be worth trading on its own technical merits.

Only Price and Volume When it comes to oscillators and indicators, I really do not have any that I religiously use on my charts. That does not mean I will not use them, because I have in the past. The problem is that I never found where using any of these stochastics, moving average convergence/divergence (MACD), relative strength indicators, or commodity channel index (CCI) indicators has provided me with any true edge in my trading that leads to increased profitability in the long term.

I do like to have some overlays, though, particularly simple moving averages in the form of the 10-day, 20-day, 50-day, and 200-day. I do not make much of them, though, and will consider them in my own technical analysis only when there is a legitimate reason to do so. Such a case would be when a stock repeatedly bounces time and time again when testing the 200-day moving average or any moving average for that matter. When I see that occur, it is usually a good indication that there is a hidden level of support that price and volume are not showing on their own. When that happens, I definitely give more weight to the moving average than I typically would. The point I am trying to make here is that I do not go out of my way looking for trading opportunities based off of the moving averages or any other indicators or oscillators for that matter.

Bollinger Bands Are Legit Another overlay that frequents my charts are Bollinger bands. I am a big fan of these, but for reasons others might not use them for. I typically just use two standard deviations for the bands, and use them primarily for determining market direction and potential reversals that could occur. Using candles on my chart, if the S&P 500 has an entire candle body outside of the upper Bollinger band, I am going to dramatically tighten up my stops on all my existing long positions. In some cases I will even sell a large chunk of my existing positions in order to minimize risk exposure.

Typically, the S&P 500 doesn't rally that well when the price has escaped the confines of the upper Bollinger band. In more instances than not, the S&P 500 will retrace within two to three days after the initial candle (in its entirety) trades outside of the upper band.

When using Bollinger bands with a setting of three standard deviations, and an entire candle body goes above the upper band (that means the opening and closing price of a stock is on the outside of the upper band), it is an automatic sell signal for me. This rarely happens, but when it does, buyer beware! I will never buy a stock under these circumstances, as it is almost always a reversal signal. Most times I will liquidate all of my holdings that I am swing trading because I am so confident in this rare phenomenon and what it means.

On the flip side, I do not give much credence to the Bollinger bands if the price action happens to go below the lower band, as it is quite common for the market to sell off well beneath the lower band for many days on end, particularly when the price action is capturing a lot of fear among traders in its move. It goes along with the old adage that says the stock market tends to take the stairs up and the elevator down. If you don't believe me, then look no further than the market recession of 2008 and the European debt crisis during the summer of 2011. The market can live outside the lower Bollinger band should it choose, but the same cannot be said of price action to the upside.

Limited Use for Other Purposes When it comes to staging entries for buying a stock or shorting a stock using Bollinger bands, do not bother with it. A lot of traders have tried, and they sound convincing when they speak of staging a buy or shorting a stock based on the price action nearing one of the bands, but I have yet to find a trader that has employed them as the centerpiece to their trading strategy and as a result succeed from it.

I simply cannot find any clear edge that would allow for me to use Bollinger bands as the primary basis for my reasoning for entering into a new position. I use Bollinger bands for managing the trade and managing risk when the situation calls for it and that is it. For everything else, I simply follow price and volume alone.

Being Cognizant of Risk and Reward

By far one of the most important concepts in trading and it goes strictly back to the "main thing" of trading, and that is "does this trade represent an acceptable probability to profit at an acceptable risk?" My stop-losses are typically in the range of 2 to 4 percent from where I get in, not because there is something magical about that stop-loss range, but more so that it is easier to find setups with appealing reward-to-risk setups when you keep the stop-loss tight.

The Risk in My Stops

For me it is a minimum of a 2-to-1 reward-to-risk play that I look for. If my average stop-loss is 3 percent, then that means I need to look for opportunities that can yield 6 percent or more. On the flip side, if my stop-loss was wider, like it was early on in my trading (sometimes as much as 10 percent in those days), I would have to look for trading opportunities that yielded a 20 percent return potential. It is much easier to take what the market gives you, and if it wants to give me 20 percent, it is going to be because I took that trade on a tight stop, and as a result it would yield me seven times the reward that I took on the risk. With a wider stop of 10 percent, it was only twice the amount risked on the trade.

Now, I know what you are going to say: "Tighter stops mean more losing trades." That is absolutely wrong! I have actually noticed my trading has improved dramatically from those early days as a result of using tighter stops. First of all, I find stops that are below key support levels for buys and above key resistance levels for shorting. That means in order to have a stop-loss within 2 to 4 percent of my entry, I have to be fairly choosy and wait for the stocks to come into that desired price range.

When I employed wider stops I tended to be much more flexible with risk and add more than I really needed to have on the trade simply because I was comfortable with losing 10 percent on a given trade. I would also be less particular about the entry price as well.

Time Element The bigger problem with this, though, is that I was spending far more time in trades that was not necessary (particularly in losing trades), and the extended time factor of the trade also increases the possibility for an unexpected news event associated with the stock. When it comes to trading, I want to spend the least amount of time in an individual trade as possible. The more time you spend, the more opportunity there is for downgrades, surprise earnings announcements, scandals, and anything else under the sun that can drive a price lower.

By keeping my stops tighter I don't have to wait as long to find out whether the trade will be a success or a failure. If I am wrong, I get in and then I get out fairly quickly, but when you use these 10 to 15 percent stop-losses like a lot of traders do, I think much of the time it is out of desperation because there is the hope that a trade will, within that wide range, eventually be proven right. The need to be proven right is the worst characteristic that you can have as a trader, and it is what often leads to capital capitulation.

One more note about stop-losses that deserves mentioning: when you keep the stop-loss tight, you are naturally going to spending less time in losing trades, and putting more of your capital in winning trades. A stock cannot go against you for very long with a tight stop in hand, before you will eventually be pushed out of the trade. On winning trades, and when the stock starts to trend in your favor, you will ensure that your capital is locked up into trades that are actually making you money and not the other way around.

Successful Trading Requires You to Wait

By having the stops tighter, you aren't necessarily taking on more losing trades as a result of the tightness in your stops, but you are being more patient and waiting longer for your entries. There is no risk in waiting. If you are waiting for a stock to come down to your price and it takes off without you, who cares? I don't. The stock has the right to do that, and I do not feel violated because it did not wait for me to get into the trade. When you feel that way, you are personalizing your trades and incorporating too much emotion into your trades. Far too often, we get caught up in what the trade is doing when we are not actually in the trade by fantasizing about all the money that we "could have" made on the trade, instead of refocusing our efforts and going after the next trading opportunity.

Embrace the Fact that You Will Lose As a trader, you have to be willing to lose. It is going to happen. As I said before, I am wrong at least 40 percent of the time and I think nothing less of myself because of it. In fact, I could be wrong more than 50 percent of the time and I would still be a successful trader. Much of that has to do with how I position myself for the trade.

Since I am waiting for the right price to come to me, and because my stops are much tighter, I find out very quickly if the trade is going to go in my favor, and if it does not, I can move on to the next trade. Because of this, I can trade at a much greater frequency because my capital is not tied up in some stock that I'm waiting for a 10 percent stop-loss to trigger on.

Capital Inventory Turnover If you are confident in your trading strategy and that statistical evidence it has produced for you over the years, and you know you are right about 55 percent of the time and average about $2 in gains for every $1 you lose, then would you rather have the opportunity to trade 10 stocks at this rate or 20? Of course, you would choose the latter, and that is why, once you get settled into your trading strategy and can consistently extract profits out of the market, you will not want to tie up your capital in do-nothing trades longer than you have to.

Instead, you want to keep your winners as long as you can without getting stopped out (but constantly doing everything you can to secure as much in profits as possible in the trade while it rises) while moving your capital from the small losing trades into the next opportunity that you can profit from. That, my friend, is how you make your money work for you and not be a slave to the need to ultimately be right in your trading efforts.

Aim Small, Miss Small

More to the point of keeping your stops tight comes the inspiration from one of my most favorite movies of all time: *The Patriot*. In the movie, Benjamin Martin is on the march through the country backwoods to free his eldest son from his British captors. He brings his two younger boys and their rifles along for the ride to provide some cover. Prior to opening fire on the enemy, he asks his sons, "What did I tell you fellas about shooting?" In unison they reply with "Aim small, miss small," after which they go on to wreak havoc and reunite with their captured brother and son.

In your trading, you should keep a similar motto when defining your risk on a trade. If your risk is contained, minimal and small, any loss you might incur will likewise be small. If your trading resembles some hellion taking a rifle and firing recklessly at anything that moves, without even taking the time to focus in the sights of the gun on the target you are aiming at, then what are the chances that you will actually be able to consistently profit in your trades and, more important, be able to close out year after year with a profit in the markets. It is not likely. So in your trading, take the risk side of the trade as seriously, in fact more seriously, than any other aspect of the trade. If you do this, the profits will take care of themselves, and that is a promise.

Hit Singles and Doubles—Not Home Runs

I like to equate the gains from winning trades to hits in baseball: singles, doubles, triples, and home runs. Everyone loves the home run trade, where you are able to bank a lifetime trade of insane profits. They do happen from time to time, but I would not "bank" on that happening all the time or even all that much. It is always the exception to the rule despite the fact most traders will kill themselves in the process of finding the holy grail for home run stocks.

Over the past 20 years, some of the biggest names in baseball have been Barry Bonds, Sammy Sosa, and Mark McGwire. They managed to tally numbers in their baseball careers as well as in single seasons that had never been matched before and probably will not be ever again. Unfortunately, though, they had something else in common: it is widely believed that all three have used performance-enhancing drugs to assist them in their home run totals.

But athletes like Cal Ripkin Jr., Ichiro, and Derek Jeter, who are much smaller guys in their body frame and stature, have never been accused of taking any performance-enhancing drugs. Unlike the home-run sluggers, they are either in the Baseball Hall of Fame in Cooperstown or they are guaranteed a placed in it one day when they retire. Despite having 1,954 home runs between them, Bonds, McGwire, and Sosa will likely never step foot into the Hall of Fame.

Jeter, Ichiro, and Cal Ripkin Jr. are well known for reaching base on a very consistent basis, sporting solid career batting averages, and coming through in the clutch when their teams needed them the most.

Reach Base When Trading

With that said, the question that is expected: what do drugs, baseball, and home runs have to do with trading stocks? A lot, actually!

Let me explain. Far too often, we swing for the fences in our trading, thinking that we can buy a certain product, follow a certain guru, or buy a certain stock and hold on to it for dear life, believing that doing so will fulfill our wildest trading fantasies of striking the "big one."

Here's an illustration as it pertains to baseball: What would you think if the batter at the plate had a 3-0 count (only needing one more ball for a walk) and instead of waiting for a pitch to come right down the middle for him to swing at (i.e., make the pitcher do the work), he starts swing at the next three wild pitches regardless of how close they are to the strike zone and subsequently strikes out. If you were a fan of the team that he played for, you would be yelling and cursing at your television set and think the guy was an idiot, wondering how he ever made his way into the starting lineup.

Trade with What the Market Pitches You But often, we do the exact same thing in our trading, where instead of taking some gains off the table, or looking to make consistent gains in the market, we instead swing for the fences despite having made a very solid trade (same thing as being up 3-0 in the count and swinging no matter the pitch's location)

Instead, you have to take some balls maybe a strike or two, but avoid swinging at everything that comes your way. If the home-run ball comes down the middle of the plate, take the swing, but for Pete's sake let it come to you—do not try to make it happen with every trade you take, and that is what so many traders do.

It is hard to be satisfied with just "getting on base" when it comes to trading. We thumb our nose at 1 or 2 percent on a given trade, and think it is not much to speak of and envision our trades being in the range of

10 to 20 percent, which is much more rare, and those who aim for those kinds of consistent returns strike out a whole lot more (just ask Babe Ruth).

As a part-time trader, you are limited by the amount of time and resources that you can devote to a stock in attempting to unearth some kind of rare gem. So do not try to do so. There are thousands of such people at the major brokerage firms with far more connections, resources, and inside tracks doing what you are trying to do on your own as a part-time trader. It simply doesn't make much sense at all. That is why I prefer technical analysis over fundamental analysis as well. As a retail trader, you have more of an advantage.

First, most brokerage firm shun the technical analysis craft, and second, it allows for retail traders such as ourselves to see where the "big money" is leaving its footprints, through the use of technical analysis.

Ask Yourself This ... So if you're frustrated by your trading, if you think you let too many winners turn into losers, or you place trades on the hype surrounding you (be it Twitter or some discussion forum), then ask yourself, in the long run, are you better off missing out on a few home-run balls and also avoiding some mega-losers, for the opportunity to consistently extract profits from this market by taking the gains that you have, and not holding out for the gains you hope for and are likely never to come your way?

Home-run hitters will definitely sell tickets, because who does not like seeing a slugger strike the ball so hard that the ball flies out of the park? It is truly something to marvel at. But what any general manager will tell you is that it is not the occasional home run that wins you a championship, but the on-base percentage of his players—the frequency with which you can get on base and score. If your on-base percentage is not at a high enough percentage, your team is not going to go very far.

As it goes, then, with your trading, your obsession should be consistently and successfully closing out winning trades at a level where the profit far outpaces the risk taken on the trade, as well as not striking out when you are up on the count (i.e., letting winners turn into losers) and, most important, having a strategy in place that keeps you from striking out too much (that is, managing risk) in hopes of getting the long ball.

This runs counter to what most will tell you, particularly those who are trying to sell you a product or service, because what they are trying to do is appeal to your vulnerabilities, hopes, and aspirations of riches and easy living. They are trying to sell you a dream. Sure, it would be nice to always strike it big with every one of our winning trades on a regular and consistent basis, but we are fooling ourselves if we think we can take that as a normal trading strategy and actually succeed in doing so.

If you are still not certain about what I have told you in this section, then just ask Jeter, Ichiro, and Ripkin. I'm sure they could tell how the simple walk, single, or double has done wonders for their career.

The Best Way to Trade at Work

If you are not going to use stops because either (1) you prefer mental stops, (2) the market makers will "steal" your shares, (3) you are afraid of it popping back up as soon as you get stopped out, or some other reason not mentioned, you are wrong—there is no excuse for not using the stops.

■ Always Use Stop-Losses

You see, small losses are okay and are very easy to recover from and that is what you want when it comes to a losing trade. Being able to put the losing trade behind you and move on to the next trade is key and using tight stops as I have discussed throughout this book is what leads you down the path to successful trading.

Stop-Loss Frustrations

There will no doubt be occasions where the market makers steal your shares or you simply get stopped out pure and simple only to witness the stock moving back up to new highs before the day is over. It is frustrating, I know. I have had it happen to me countless times, but that is part of the game, and trust me, I would rather take a small loss from someone who wants to take my shares at a cheap price, than let one of these stocks rip me a new one because my ego was so big that I had to control my losses by a means other than a stop-loss, namely, some belief that I would know before it was too late that I needed to get out of the trade.

When it does happen, though, and traders get stopped out of their trade early on, it is easy to become discouraged. In general, when I am stopped out of a trade, I do not even bother looking at the price action in the stock anymore. My stop-loss placement is such that when it is hit, there is something technically contrary for my original reasons for trading it. As a result, once that stop-loss is hit, I trust my analysis and move on, not allowing for the stock to occupy any of my thoughts going forward.

Avoid Hindsight Being fallible as a human, if I watch a stock rip higher after I had been stopped out or just sold my shares in general, it adds nothing to my plate nor helps my trading to witness the stock's action after the fact. A stock is bound to go up or down after we get out of it, and since there are only two options for a stock to take, why should I allow myself to get upset or frustrated simply because the stock is moving in some direction after I get out?

I also do not want to see a stock that reverses course and crashes after I get out at the peak (capturing peak profits is not a regular occurrence for me or any other trader for that fact), because I may grow overly confident that I might have some kind of psychic powers that allows me to foretell the future of a stock price's movement. Such an attitude can also be detrimental to one's trading.

Getting stopped out early on, though, and watching the stock run without the trader in the pilot's seat can cause discouragement and allow for the trader to become leery of using stop-losses and instead rely on their own instincts and discernment for determining when to cut the losses when they inevitably occur. This is probably the worst decision that one can make and can take you out of the game faster than you can imagine.

Suck It Up I am here to tell you that getting stopped out of trades is a part of life. Furthermore, getting stopped out of a trade prematurely only for it to go on a major run soon thereafter is also going to happen to you as long as you trade with stops (which I hope you will always do). The sooner you come to grips with this reality, the better off you will be. The use of stop-losses is not a perfect science. Every time you get stopped out does not necessarily mean that the stock you are trading in is going into the crapper (though we would all like for that to be the case). Instead, you should be placing your stops at a strategic point on the chart that should the price of the stock hit your stop, you know that there is a strong or likely possibility that the behavior of the stock itself is diverging from the thesis that propelled you to buy the stock in the first place. When that happens, you should actually want to get out of the stock.

It is also worth noting that just because you get stopped out does not mean that you can't get back in, but there has to be a reason for jumping back in. Probably 95 percent of the trades I get stopped out of, I never get right back into. Most of the time it is just a trade that did not work out and I move on. Nonetheless, my stop is, in essence, an insurance policy from a stock blowing up my portfolio and taking me out of the game, as well as protecting me from myself. But as long as I manage my risk and therefore my losses, I stay in the game and allow myself the chance to experience success on the next trade.

Use Position Sizes that Won't Be Distracting to You

There was a time while in the corporate world where I had a little more time on my hands than I typically would, so I thought I it would be a great idea to expand my trading into futures. Keep swing trading successfully as I always had, but now add a new a new element to my trading strategy: futures trading.

In my opinion, anything that can be charted and where technical analysis can be used, I believe, can be traded. Futures were no different. The only problem with futures, though, was that I was far too distracted by the position sizes. I was primarily trading the S&P 500 e-mini contracts and in doing so was scalping the index for small gains to the tune of one- to-two point moves.

Future Distractions

Not only were the positions distracting, the system I had developed was distracting for me and my job as well. I relied on intraday signals that were unpredictable in nature, in regard to when they would actually fire off. I could go to a meeting and miss five or six trades in a one-hour period and not get another alert the rest of the day. Nonetheless, I pushed forward. What was even more distracting was how annoying it was to everyone I worked with.

When I had a signal to buy a position in the e-mini S&P 500 contract, it would be based off a certain set of parameters that indicated the market was oversold and ready for the bounce. As a result, my trade alert signal was Charlie Brown saying "Oh, good grief" in the most depressing of ways. However, when the markets were rallying hard and ready for a pullback, *Toy Story*'s Buzz Lightyear would come to life and say, "To infinity . . . and beyond!"

This was not just annoying me, it was annoying everyone in the office. It was incredibly distracting for me from a work perspective as well because every time one of those blasted alerts went off, I had to react immediately, and it could really interrupt the flow of assignments that I was working on for my actual job. Now my office mates had no idea what I was up to. It never occurred to them that I had created some sophisticated trading system alerting me to buy and sell signals.

Instead, they just thought I had modified my e-mail system to where each time I received a new e-mail, Buzz Lightyear or Charlie Brown would let their voice be heard. I did not try to change their opinion of this at all. I figured it was best for me and them that they did not know the true reasons for those cartoon characters coming to life in the workplace.

Priorities Became Jumbled It would not be unusual for me to be in someone else's office talking to someone about an important matter, to hear Buzz Lightyear's voice ring through the air. Upon hearing it, I would cut off any conversation we might have been having and would make a hurried beeline back to my office to place the trade that Buzz called for. Make no mistake about it—this became a huge disruption for me and my job. I found myself watching the charts even when I did not have a trade on or even alerted. I was trying to anticipate the trade.

Despite the distraction it was creating for me, I was extremely successful trading the futures contracts. I had a method to my madness and it was working for me, but the interference with my job priorities was putting me at risk to where if I stayed on this path, the problems it would create with the boss man would far outweigh the measured success trading futures I was experiencing. I was only three months into trading this strategy, but the profits, while nice, were not big enough that that I could simply quit my job, nor would I want to, based on a three-month futures track record.

Even more distracting became the position sizes. While I was not taking on outsized large positions, futures in their very nature carry a lot of risk, because of each individual contract value and the level of margin that is required for each trade. I always used stop-losses on the trades, but because the position sizes were large simply due to the general nature of trading futures,

I was not willing to leave my desk while I had a trade under way nor could I go to meetings or focus my efforts on other activities I should have been working on.

A lot of it was paranoia. I knew that if I went off to a meeting, I would always assume the worst: my stop-loss was put in incorrectly, and a meteorite hit planet Earth, wiping out half the world's population, and the markets subsequently crashed, taking my entire position with it. By being in front of my computer I could spare myself the fear of the worst case scenario taking place and my not being around to act accordingly in response.

Good System, Bad Environment Some of you might be shaking your head while reading this and saying, "Here you had a system you could trade, you were doing good at it, and you let yourself get in the way of it." Quite frankly, I would not disagree with you on this assessment either. I would follow up that thought with my own, and that is trading is about finding a system that fits your personality, your circumstances, and your risk profile. Trading futures intraday on an alert system that I had created while at work was by far moronic to the *n*th degree.

My personality was not geared to trading futures in the manner I had created it for. I found myself trying to anticipate trades, and though I might have gotten away with trading like this in my work environment, eventually it would have caught up with me. I could not trade at work with Buzz and Charlie sounding the alarm bell 6 to 10 times in a given day, not to mention the missed alerts I would experience due to having to be in meetings, on travel, or some other reason beyond my control. Finally, I was constantly worried and paranoid about a black-swan event taking place that could have rendered my portfolio useless, and, consequently, I would often find myself stressed out and unable to concentrate on my responsibilities on the job, so then it clearly did not fit my personality.

Often, traders will buy someone else's system for trading at a premium price thinking that because the system works for that individual, it will most definitely work for them as well and eliminate any doubt otherwise. However, within that system are all sorts of complicated elements that the original trader to the system understands and is comfortable with, but nearly every person who tries to duplicate his efforts fails miserably. Assuming that the system is legitimate and not some sham (like many of them are), the most likely cause for the failure lies in the purchaser of that system because the system does not fit his environment, personality, or risk profile (in some cases all three).

The SharePlanner Investment System

Over the years I designed a trading system to try to meet the personality of the typical part-time trader. Understanding that the person may not be able to watch the markets from opening bell to closing bell like the full-time traders can, I created a system that minimizes research time by only sending out 40 to 50 trade alerts each year (sometimes more), using a position sizing system that is designed around the trader's personality (the default risk profile is 10 percent position sizes, but you can make it more or less depending on your risk profile). Obviously, I wanted a system that could outperform the S&P 500; otherwise, what would be the point of trading my system if it did not beat the market (otherwise you would just buy the SPY ETF)?

Designed for Simplicity and Duplicity

The next and final aspect of the system was to manage risk in a way that did not create uneasiness among its traders. In doing so, I limited the system to trade only those stocks listed in the S&P 500 and no other. The other half of the risk management was to always use a trailing stop-loss of 10 percent that gave the system enough room for the investment to play itself out. This may sound contradictory to how I swing trade stocks for a living when my average stop-loss is 24 percent from my entry price. It is different because my investment system has its average position last three to four months at a time, whereas my swing trading is looking for positions that last a max of a couple of weeks.

My investment system only has 40 to 50 trades, whereas my swing trading has well over 250 trades per year. So the contrasts are startling because the approach to investing in stocks long-term versus swing trading on a short-term basis is startling as well.

Simplicity was a huge factor in creating my investment system because I knew traders could not be on standby like I was when trading futures waiting to place seven or eight trades each session. Therefore, I made it where the investment picks, where there was one on a given day, would be sent out before the market opens. Then to top it off, the goal of the system is to not to wait around to use one's discretion of when they should buy the stock. Instead, the system dictates that the purchase should be made as soon as the market opens.

Works Around Your Job

What I created was a trading system that should have a low level of conflict with most traders' personalities and their job responsibilities. The biggest criticism that I receive is that they wish the investment system was more active, but if you want that, you are better off subscribing to my swing-trading alerts.

Investments, by their very name, are always going to be less in frequency. On the risk front the investment system will not ruffle a lot of feathers. Sure, there will be stocks that get stopped out just like any system has, but at the end of the day, the volatility is much less than what you would see in just about every other newsletter on the planet. Keeping the part-time trader in mind, the SharePlanner Investment System is geared toward the working environment of Corporate America, while also striving to be personality and risk profile friendly. If you have not tried it out yet, I would highly encourage you to do so at SharePlanner.com.

Plan Your Trade and Trade Your Plan

It was once said about Don Shula, whom I regard as one of the greatest coaches of all time in any sport, that he could take his and beat yours, or he could take yours and beat his. It was not about having the all the right players at all the positions, but it was because he knew how to coach and use whatever resources he had been given. On most sports teams, there is a general manager and a head coach that represent two different people (in some cases, the head coach acts as the general manager). As a result of this arrangement, the general manager is responsible for finding the right people on the team, and the head coach is responsible for coaching them. Shula coached and did that by not being consumed with the players he was given by management. Instead, he focused his efforts on managing his players and coaching them right. He was confident enough in his coaching skills that it did not matter whether he had his players or yours; he would beat you either way.

More About the Management, Not the Stock

The same should be said of our trading. Our long-term success as a trader is not going to be dictated by how well we pick winning stocks, and stocks that make us huge profits. Instead, it will depend on how well we manage those trades that we are given. You see, the market is our general manager. It gives us the trades that we can manage on any given day. You cannot argue with the market because you only have the responsibly of a coach, and in this case, you are the coach of your portfolio. How well the stocks do depends on how well you manage them and put them in a position that will allow you to succeed.

Not About the Stock Far too many traders concern themselves with the "pick." In the classes that I teach in the SharePlanner Academy, I tell the traders that when it comes to about 95 percent of all the traders out there, I could take my trades and beat their trades, and then on the flip side, I could take their trades that they take and beat my own trades that I would have have traded had I let them be at the helm. It comes across as arrogant, I know, but it is not because I am some kind of genius; rather, it is because I go through the painstaking efforts to make sure that I manage the trade in general and the risk in particular.

Count the Dollars Later That is my focus and not the actual hope of what the stock might do after I get in the trade. I am able to do much better than the average Joe in trading, regardless of what stocks I am trading with. Once you start asking yourself, "If the stock goes up $5 per share, that means I will have made "X" dollars, you have already lost on the trade. Like Kenny Rogers said in the song *The Gambler*, "You never count your money when you're sitting at the table, there'll be time enough for countin' when the dealing's done."

Going through the "what if" dollar scenarios of what future gains might be like is a losing battle. Once you have gotten to that point, whether it is during market hours or not, your focus is off of the trade itself and your mind is now in fantasy land trying to dash forward to what the trade might ultimately do to your advantage. If you are having trouble with this issue, then shift your focus to what you will do if the stock goes against you and how you will manage the trade going forward, and at which point, if the trade is profitable, you will want to move the stop-loss up to and why. This is truly the mindset of the successful part-time and full-time trader alike. Leave Fantasy Land to Disney World tourists, and consume yourself with the trade's risk management.

Expecting the Worse You could say I have a "prove otherwise" kind of attitude in my approach to trading. I expect the trade to go wrong. I never take it for granted and enter the trade with the predisposition that the trade will result in being a loser. That is not because of some lack of self-esteem in my own trading abilities because I have traded long enough to know what I am capable of as a trader. Instead, it has everything to do with my approach to trading stocks, and my concerns not with whether I will win in a trade, but how I will manage the trade in any and all situations that I am confronted with.

Don Shula was a great football coach for the Miami Dolphins not because he drafted great players but because he was great at managing them. He knew how to extract every ounce of talent and potential out of them and then put a plan together that allowed them to win on Sundays. It is not necessary that you can beat people with their own picks, as stated earlier, but instead, I want you to become consumed with the management of each trade and making sure nothing goes haywire on you that would ultimately compromise your ability to profit consistently from your trading and the market.

Your players are your trades, and making sure that you extract the potential in each trade is your duty. Not making a self-inflicted mistake that could have been otherwise avoidable is absolutely necessary to ensure the long-term profits that you seek.

■ The 90/10 Rule

Further to the point of managing the trade, 90 percent of successful trading in the financial markets has to do with the management and planning of the trade. There is probably only 10 percent of the trade that is actually tied into the stock itself. Managing the trade has everything to do with it. To expand on the Don Shula analogy, I am quite confident that you can experience a relative degree of certain success by placing all of the liquid and tradable stocks in a hat and randomly drawing a stock out of it and then trading it, as long as you have a plan for the trade and manage it as you should. By saying that I sound like I am challenging the notion that stocks and their movement results in nothing but randomness and that whether a stock goes up or down has nothing to do really with the stock itself.

That is not what I am saying at all, though. The point that I want to make is that stocks will rise and fall on their own merit, including growth, earnings, revenues, technical analysis, and so on. As traders, we are trying to be successful managers of stocks. Realize that the aforementioned traits all play into a stock's movement, but your ability to trade successfully is not going to be based on how a stock trades after earnings, whether they get FDA approval for their latest drug in development, or the random upgrade/downgrade issued by one of the brokerage firms. The management of the trade comes down to the pretrade studies and screens that you conduct, the entry price you decide upon, the market direction of the broader markets, and how you will trade off of them.

Above All Else … Manage

Once you are in the trade, successfully implement your plan, which includes getting in at the desired entry price and putting on a stop loss according to your analysis. If the stock goes against you, then you will want to make sure that your order executes at your stop-loss, and if the trade goes in your favor, you will need to proactively manage the profits to prevent a winner from turning into a loser.

It is so much more than finding that *"it"* stock that somehow does all the work for you. Even when someone does buy into the stock that rips higher and higher, often the trader is so scared about booking gains, as if it might be some kind of sin to do so, that instead of booking what can be rightfully his, he will watch that trade ultimately come all the way back down to where it first started, and then drop even further. I've seen it time and time again.

I know two people who slaved away at desk jobs during the 1990s' dot-com bubble, yet managed to buy Sun Microsystems (now JAVA) and Qualcomm when they were trading for pennies on the dollar, then rose to astronomical prices, and they both practically became overnight millionaires, if they had simply put in a "sell order" to book those gains. But they did not do so. Instead, they were so afraid of selling out of fear that the stock might go higher still without them, and that was a chance that they were willing to bet their millions in profits on; in doing so, they lost it all. One of them actually is holding out hope that one day JAVA will return to its glory days like the prodigal child he unfortunately believes it to be.

Why do I even bother with technical analysis then? The answer is simple: it can give us an edge by which we can exert the 90 percent of the effort toward managing. There is absolute worth in technical analysis, but it is a useless exercise if you do not have discipline and a willingness to manage the trade. The charts provide you with the road map by which you can manage the trade, which includes defining the ideal entry to get in on and defining the reward and potential of a trade, while also determining where below resistance you are going to place your stop-loss once you get long or short on the trade. The technical analysis might be only a small factor of the trade, but it is still much needed because it is what the 90 percent management factor is based on.

The Door and Its Hinges

Take a door, for example. A typical door opens and closes and does what you want it to do, but the only reason it can do that is the three tiny hinges that allows it to go back and forth. Those hinges happen to be your stock, and the door, which represents nearly the entire apparatus, represents the management of the trade.

You need a stock that gives you an acceptable probability to profit at an acceptable level of risk. Without the door you have a set of hinges that serve no purpose, and with no hinges you have a door that can't stand on its own. So it goes with trading—if you do not manage the trade, your stock picks are useless, but your management can work only as long as there is a stock that provides you with the parameters that have been detailed throughout this chapter.

There is no doubt that you can trade if you apply the principles in this book to your trading. But while I provide you with the way to become a successful part-time trader, you have to be willing to follow the road map in order to get there. It is not simply about finding some stocks and throwing some money at them, thinking you can just sit back and watch them grow. Like crops in the field, you have to diligently tend to the garden, and if you plan on reaping the profits, you better take care of your crops until the harvest comes.

PART III

BECOMING THE PART-TIME TRADER

CHAPTER 11

Trading Habits You Will Want to Avoid

There is a great sense of urgency to get to our final destination in trading, as if there actually is one. The fact of the matter is that trading the financial markets is ever changing and the education never ceases to end. You will always find yourself learning how to trade better and constantly having to adjust to the challenges that the stock market presents you with. So the idea that there is some kind of final state that a trader reaches in his or her progression is a complete fallacy. Over time, if you apply yourself to the principles that I have outlined in this book, you will no doubt get better, and as you experience and see more out of the financial markets, your ability to trade better will increase likewise.

Learning from My Shortcomings

The concepts that I have outlined in this book, the "Do's and Don'ts," come primarily from my own shortcomings as a trader. I have made more mistakes as a trader than you could ever imagine, but I am a successful trader today because of those experiences and the learning curve I had to experience to get where I am today. I have also had to learn to trade despite personality traits of my own that can get in the way of my successfully trading. Trading is hard work and any attempt to cut short the learning progression and experience that is necessary to equip you, the individual trader, for success, will be met with disastrous results.

A part of the financial industry that truly enrages me are all of these trading courses that sell you on the promise that if you spend the thousands of dollars that their course costs, you can make the same millions of dollars that they were able to make. They also use the element of time to appeal to your need to buy their course. They will do it over five days and somehow in just those five days you will magically become self-aware about all things trade related and therefore ready to take on the markets with all of these secrets that you have been equipped with.

Let me just tell you something, if they are trying to sell you their secrets to success, they are not secrets, they are well-known facts and in some cases, well-known fallacies, and nothing that you will ultimately benefit from.

Seek Improvement, Not Solutions The education that I have provided through the SharePlanner Academy over the years has not been to provide a stop-gap measure, all-in-one solution for traders to miraculously go from the beginning trader to one with expert knowledge. Not even close. Instead, my academy is there to help you along your journey.

Your approach to educating yourself should be to teach you different concepts and theories, strategies and understandings when it comes to trading and doing it successfully. When someone completes one of my courses, I expect them to get better, assuming that they apply what they have been taught, but it is not, nor will it ever be, your holy grail to trading success.

If you are going to become the trader you want to become, it is going to be because you took the time and paid your dues in becoming that trader. We look at skill sets like playing the violin or learning to tickle the ivories on the piano or strum out a melody on a guitar, and not for a moment does one believe that the professionals who plays this instrument achieved their success overnight, or bought some course that took them from unskilled and into someone who was ready for the London Symphony Orchestra. Not a chance. Instead, they learned to play their musical instrument through blood, sweat, and tears, by studying every facet of that instrument, and learning the theories behind them and how to play musical numbers of increasing difficulty. Then and only then, after years of experience did they finally get there.

Traders and Athletes Alike Take professional athletes, for example. Did former Miami Dolphins quarterback Dan Marino just suddenly walk on the field one day and become the starting quarterback for the Miami Dolphins? More so, what about Peyton Manning, who is well known for practicing when no one else is practicing, and studying every game film he could get his hands on of his opponents, so that he would know every facet of the game. I can assure you that what they did not do was go on the Internet and find someone who said if they bought their quarterbacking videos, they would somehow be ready for the NFL.

These great athletes started when they were just little kids, wearing shoulder pads that were wider than they were tall. By the time they reached the professional level, they had eight years of experience just at the high school and college level under their belt, not to mention all of the time they spent in the little leagues.

No Quick Fix in Trading The same goes for trading, too. We simply believe that we can watch a couple of videos, buy a few penny stocks, and suddenly be rich like Warren Buffett. It simply is not possible. But, of course, most of those trading web sites that promise instant success and exotic riches will trot out personal testimonials, both written and filmed in tropical locations, showing you how their customers have benefited from their service and gotten rich in the process. Know this, though— most of these testimonials are false. That's right, they are false. People do not actually say that. They are either part of the company, a friend, or paid to come up with garbage testimonials to convince you that they are true and legit.

What you have to do is come to grips with the prospect that it will take years and years to get to where you want to be with trading, and even when you think you have arrived you still have an endless journey ahead, as you have only scratched the surface. There are no shortcuts, but there are plenty of good resources that you can take advantage of to help assist you in your trading endeavors and your progression over time.

Stay Away from Trades that Force You to Dip into Margin

Another shortcut that traders like to take is overleveraging themselves in hopes that having more money to trade will lead to more profits to be had. I have seen traders max out credit cards, take out lines of credit on their house, deplete their savings, and even take a penalty on their 401(k) just to gain access to additional funds. That is a huge red flag, and the primary motivation that arises from these actions is greed, and underneath that greed I would not be surprised if there was a huge addiction to gambling as well, whether that person realizes it or not.

Avoid Catastrophes

Remember, when you are trading, you are doing everything you can to not create a major setback, because even just one major event can mean that you work even more years on the job and for someone else's benefit. Keeping that in mind, do not push the envelope just because you can. With most margin accounts, you can be matched dollar for dollar in terms of how much capital can be committed to one trade.

Let's say that you took advantage of every last dollar you had available for trading, meaning you were 200 percent long in your portfolio. Let's also say you have an average stop-loss of 5 percent from each of your entries on your positions. Assume as well that the market had one of those unusual days where you were in high-beta stocks, and there was a 4 percent market pullback, which was enough to stop you out of each of your positions. For an account that was fully capitalized in the market, that would be a significant setback of 5 percent in losses across your entire portfolio. But because you were 200 percent long using the margin that was available, you lost 10 percent of your account value in just one day, and just to get back to your original starting point, you will have to make 11.1 percent against your existing capital. Depending on what type of market you have on your hands, that can take months to get back.

Leveraging Has Much More Downside to It Trading is difficult, and the last thing you want to do is bury yourself in a hole that you spend most of your trading year in just trying to crawl out, at which point, if you are lucky enough to survive the psychological impact it has on your trading, you will only break even, still needing to increase your portfolio value in the limited amount of time that you have left in the year.

So stay away from the use of margin. I'm not saying that there is not ever a reason to go into margin. I personally draw the line when I am 100 percent vested in the market, but I do think the large majority of traders have no business dipping into margin one bit. Since you are trading while on the job, the last thing you want to do is begin leveraging yourself and your account to the point where, if the market goes against you, the emotions are magnified and the frustrations increased unnecessarily. That kind of trading environment coupled with the pressures of your job will lead to your making a decision you otherwise would not make.

An Emotional Spasm

In the primitive years of my trading while still in the corporate world, I became increasingly frustrated by some of the decisions management was making. I had stellar reviews each year and was a valued member of my organization (still during that time when I was actually considered a "rising star"). I had been around for a few years and been promoted once, but then I started noticing they were bringing in these know-nothing, new grads into the organization at a pay rate about 20 percent higher than the salary I was being paid. Pandemonium ensued. Meetings—of my own doing, actually—were held, and the "we'll take an 'action' to look into that" statements were proclaimed, which is typically no better than someone telling you to "get a life, you're not worth our time!"

It ultimately took three different bosses and a couple years of my life to get the salary adjustment I deserved, and, of course, by that time, inflation had made it where I was just making a new-grad salary despite my not being so newly graduated.

Speeding Up the Process

I felt like I had to take matters into my own hands. I was not going to sit around and let the boss man screw around with me and all these years of my life, just hoping to garner the attention of management, thinking that they would come around to paying me what I was really worth. As a result of all this corporate baloney, I decided to use some of the money I had in a line of credit against our home. It was exciting at first. It was not a lot of money, but at the time I did not have that big a trading account and was in the primitive stages of seeing the portfolio increase in size. Before, I only had enough capital to trade two or so stocks at a time. Now, all of a sudden, I had the ability to trade up to eight stocks at a time.

"Just imagine how awesome it would be to make all that money in all eight stocks instead of just two stocks," I thought to myself, and at this point, mistakes are already starting to pile up on me, just by the mere thought.

Pitfalls Out of the Gate First, I was trading with money that I was not comfortable trading with and money that should never be used in conjunction with trading. Second, I was trading with more positions than I had become accustomed to trading. I had been used to trading only one or two positions at a time, and now all of a sudden I was increasing it to eight overnight. That was moronic on my part. Finally, I started to fantasize about what might happen, once all these positions were profitable for me. Here I was, overly confident, thinking that my newbie success was scalable without nearly enough experience under my belt.

I was literally trading with the odds stacked against me, even though I was ready to throw a party on my own behalf without having placed the first trade using the additional capital.

Once the newly acquired capital was transferred to my account, I proceeded to place seven new trades right away. I was already in one trade as it was, so this brought my total up to eight in all. The first day went well, and I was doing well. I was riding cloud nine under the belief that it was all coming together for me and I would discard that measly paycheck they thought was adequate and finally be trading on my own.

Panic Ensues

That was Monday. On Tuesday, the market opened down 1 percent. Those eight positions I had were all long positions. I started using the breathing techniques typical of what is taught to a pregnant lady in labor in hopes that I would avoid hyperventilating. This money I was losing was not my own; it came from my line of credit, and all that early success that I was experiencing might be down the toilet for me. While I hoped the market would pull a reversal on my behalf, the market declined my request and simply headed further south. Toward the final hour of trading, I had had it. With my bottom lip quivering, I sold out of all eight positions and took my lumps in the process.

In hindsight, the money was not all that much, but I was experiencing losses that I was not used to experiencing. It was the worst trading day of my life, and while I have had far worse since then (from a dollar standpoint) and handled them as part of the job of a trader, at that time I was not equipped. When I was putting all that new capital into my account, it never crossed my mind that I might actually lose on the trades, and to make matters worse, this was the second time I had made such a bone-headed move in my trading career. You'd think I would have learned my lesson the first time.

I thought I would be banking the coin on all eight positions that I could take on at a time. My experience, expectations, and knowledge that I had as a trader were ill-equipped for the trading environment I was entering into. I was so rattled I could not focus on my job the least bit. I was roughed up big time emotionally, doubted myself as a trader, and just thought of myself as being "plain stupid." I went down to the warehouse where all the shipments came in; at this time of day, they were all gone already, and I just carved out a hole in between all the boxes and pouted for the next hour or so.

Adding Insult to Injury After I was done, I had to find my way over to the IT service area (good thing I knew somebody there!) and asked my buddy Greenwood for another mouse and keyboard. The keyboard was missing a few keys, since after I slammed the right half of the keyboard on the edge of my desk while holding the other half, keys had gone everywhere. I also needed a mouse because after I closed out of my trades, I decided to put the exclamation point on my fouled-up trading day by repetitively slamming it on the table as well, to the point where the mouse's internal organs were rattling all around inside.

Of course, I did not throw my hissy-fit in a vacuum, so when all of this took place, three people came by my office (at least I had my own office with a door at this time) asking me what happened or if everything was okay. Looking disheveled, with hair that looked like it was done by Conan O'Brien's hair stylist, I simply responded with, "Yeah, why? Did you guys hear something?"

I'm sure I sold them on the believability of that response of mine, but hey, at least Greenwood upgraded my mouse to one of those with the fancy scrolling wheel on it.

Do Not Do It for the Money

Those who are considered to be at the top of their line of work, whether it be engineering, medicine, law, professional sports, the military, or any other kind of profession, are the best because they have a passion for what they do. Not because of the money, but because there is an inherent passion that drives them to succeed in such a way that it does not even feel like work.

For the Love of the Game

If you were to ask them why they do what they do, they would likely respond with an answer that does not involve money. Often, it links back to their fascination of their studies or a type of deep-rooted childhood love for their work, or the hope to be the best at what they do, none of which involves money. But what they do have that leads to their success is the passion and drive to be the best, and it is not some fallback option that they stumbled across and thought, "Hey, I can make some nice money doing this." If that is the case, they will usually burn out in very short order, or ultimately sabotage their own success with a decision or action that was primarily motivated by greed.

One of the main reasons why so many traders fail is that they enter their profession for the money. They see how simple the concept of "Buy Low, Sell High" is, and it entices the fancy of those wanting to make some quick and easy money. Their passion is not for the financial markets and specifically the craft of trading. Instead, their passion is for the money. Those kinds of people are better off in Las Vegas because they'll probably end up losing their money just like they most certainly will in the stock market, but at least they'll be able to stay in a five-star hotel and get free drinks in the process.

Your Heart Has to Be in It Unfortunately, the stock market offers no such perks. As a trader, then, you have to ask yourself whether your motivation for trading is to make money or to really be a great trader. If you seek after the latter, and apply yourself to the principles that allow a trader to succeed, then the profits will be a benefit of the profession you are dedicated to. Just like the athletes who are so well trained and skilled and dedicated to what they do, the money and multimillion-dollar contracts are simply a fruit of their labor. The moment they start playing only for the money, and not to win or be the best, the likelihood increases that they will be in the unemployment line looking for work sooner rather than later.

I love trading and every darn thing about it. There are various aspects of trading that I do not enjoy as well, but the whole experience of it I am passionate about. Writing this book has been something that I have thoroughly enjoyed because I get to take the knowledge that I have accrued over the years and put it to pen and paper and help others in the process with their own shortcomings as a trader in hopes that it makes them realize their dreams and aspirations of full-time trader status.

The greed for money and that being the compelling reason for entering into the world of trading is what will ultimately be your Waterloo. Instead of trading positions based on the analysis you conduct, you will be watching the dollar value of your positions.

When losing money becomes too painful on an individual trade, and that happens primarily with those whose focus is on making quick money, they will not take the loss on the trade like they should and instead pull some crazy stunt like doubling- or tripling-down on a position or remove their stop-losses, and allow a short-term trade to turn into a long-term investment. In the end, they wind up broke and without a chance.

■ Winning Trades Turning into Losers—The Ultimate Performance Killer

Far too often, traders allow what should be winning trades that are holding some or a lot of profits to turn into losers. Instead of taking what the market gives them, they hold out hope, believing that the stock can go higher, and the thought of that happening without still having a position in the stock causes them to take on unnecessary risks by holding stocks for far too long. Sometimes, traders even believe that the profit that they are holding is not worth worrying about because it is so small or, worse, meaningless.

Protect the Gains

As in football, you want to come away with something when you are in scoring range. Not every drive results in a touchdown, and sometimes you have to settle for a field goal. Field goals are not sexy, and neither are "small profits," but they both keep putting points on the board.

I like to draw the comparison of allowing a winner to turn into a loser to the football terminology of throwing a "Pick-Six." There is nothing worse, in football, than watching your team drive all the way down the field only to see your quarterback throw a sideline pass into the oncoming hands of a defensive back, who takes it 100 yards the other way for a touchdown of his own. Even though they scored only 7 points, it is as if they scored 14 instead, because they negated the 7 points the opposing team was about to put on the board and replaced it with 7 of their own.

I would be lying if I said I did not give this concept a lot of thought after watching my beloved Miami Dolphins repeat the same scenario over and over again throughout the years. I started to equate it to trading when my own winners would turn into losers, and so I started putting a lot more worth on taking small gains, despite not having done that before (previously, I would snub my nose at the notion of a minimal gain on a trade).

These days, I am just as thrilled about avoiding a loss with a small gain as I am about a 10 percent winner on a trade that went in my favor right out of the gate. Trading is a game of inches; sure, you will have times where you cash in on some huge winners, but the real battle is in the trenches and managing those trades that totter between stopping out and closing out the trade with a slight gain.

Small Gains Are Equally Important Over the course of a year, you can have hundreds of these kinds of trades, and if you just throw the small gains out the window and make no attempt to protect and proactively manage even the smallest of gains, thereby allowing the trade to ultimately stop out, you will be shocked at how devastating the impact is on your portfolio.

Losing that which was once profitable is downright disgusting, and should be avoided as much as humanly possible. Now, you are never going to be perfect, but I would encourage you to go back and look at your trades from the past year and find out which trades were winners that reversed course and turned into losers and how that could have been avoided, and in particular, which trades you had the obvious opportunity to come away with just a small profit on. Then look at the impact it and all the others combined would have had to your trading results. I am certain you will be shocked at what you find.

Do whatever you have to do, even at the expense of missing the home-run trade from time to time, to guard those profits that you have and treat the small gain that prevented you from being stopped out just as significant as the trades you struck it big on.

Avoid Trading Heavily in Penny Stocks

One final thought, and this is one of those shortcuts that will destroy every hope and dream you ever have of becoming a full-time, self-sufficient trader, and that is by entering the world of penny stocks. The volatility in this world is far worse than any 3X exchange-traded fund (ETF) offered on the market, and just as easily, traders are sucked into the lure of the potential for ungodly sums of money. Stop-losses simply do not work. If you use them, you have to place them so far away from the entry price that getting stopped out, even on a semiregular basis, will destroy your portfolio.

When a stock trades in the pennies, there is a reason for it: they are high-risk companies whose chances for survival are slim-to-none. There are so many scandals, scams, and schemes in this world that to jump into the world of fraudsters only lets you feed out of their hands.

I am not even going to get any further into the penny stocks discussion. As you can see from my earlier discussion about my own experiences, the only thing that needs to be said here about this realm of trading is to not venture into it.

Road Bumps Ahead

All in all, there are plenty of obstacles out there to derail your trading success—even more so as a part-time trader because often there is such a sense of urgency to become that full-time trader and to do so by taking some of the dangerous shortcuts that seem all too alluring. Remain steady, though; do not give in, and do not become dismayed.

Trading is a long journey, and if you remain dedicated to sound trading principles and not circumventing the progress that you are making, I am quite confident you will make it. The key is to keep your head in the game, to avoid getting bored, and trying to become more creative on how you can speed up the process.

If you thought it was boring as a part-time trader, at least you had another job you could do; full-time trading, unless you are constantly scalping the market for small gains, will make you want to pick up a side hobby of some kind just to help pass the time. No matter how bored you get, though, do not take any shortcut that, on the surface, would appear to shorten your education. If you do, it will only add years to your part-time trading career.

CHAPTER 12

You Still Have to Get Your Real Work Done

I suppose our part-time trading endeavors would be ideal if we could just push aside the real work that ultimately hinges on whether we stick around or are kicked to the curb by the boss man, and focus solely on the trading aspect that so easily attracts our attention. If we could do that, though, we would not really be part-time traders but full-time traders. If you think about it, the fact that you bought this book called *The Part-Time Trader* presupposes your acknowledgment that you are or are wanting to be a part-time trader and understand that you still have to get done the work that pays the bills and puts food on the table.

Emotions on the Job

What we think and what we do can be at odds with each other. I always knew I needed to get my work done, but when I had a bad day trading, I could become very demotivated in my job responsibilities to where I simply neglected what I needed to be doing as it pertained to my job. When I had a really good day in the markets, I was in such a state of euphoria that I would compare my daily earnings from the market to what I was making in my 9-to-5 job and found utter contempt for the amount of labor that was given to the latter and amount earned in doing so. There were days where I could more than earn in one trading session what I made in a given week on the job. It was quite difficult to remain motivated in that regard.

Find a Middle Ground

Neither of these scenarios is healthy for balancing part-time trading with successful job management. Sure, it's okay to feel good about a successful day in the financial markets—it is only human—but in order to balance it with a full-time job, you have to manage the emotions in such a way that it does not put you in the management crosshairs for neglecting your job responsibilities.

It can be hard, though, when you want to get out of your job so badly that a typical day where you lose a small portion of your capital trading in the markets can weigh a lot heavier on the psyche because you realize that it is going to be that much longer that you have to stay in the corporate fold.

Planning Around Meetings

There are plenty of obstacles that can get in your way on the path to being that full-time trader that sheds the bindings of Corporate America. If there was one aspect of my job that I hated more than any other, it was meetings. I can say with near certainty that I did not need to be at 95 percent of all the meetings that I was required to attend. In most meetings I had nothing to offer, and when I did, there was someone more senior that they would rather listen to instead. More times than not, I sat in those meetings and just let my imagination run wild about anything but work.

Meeting Distraction

One particular time, I was in a meeting, and thank goodness for that laptop approval, because I was finally able to take something with me to these meetings to help pass the time. More often than not, I would watch the markets during the meetings, as long as I was able to sit at a corner of the conference table and angle myself in such a way that no one else could see my screen at all.

This particular time, though, I remember watching ESPN baseball highlights, and sometimes these videos would just start up all on their own. At this point in the meeting, I had about 20 windows running on my screen, when I had one of those rare occasions where I was asked to speak on a particular subject involving our organization. About halfway through my labored response, I hear, "*Vladimir Guerrero up to bat . . . back, back, back, BOOM GOES THE DYNAMITE!!! Three-run homer for Vladdy!*"

The funniest thing about this is that it had not dawned on me that it was my computer airing the audio for all to hear. Instead, I was looking around the room wondering if someone was going to mute their volume. I finally realized that it was in fact me, and it was that awkward moment where everybody in the room knew it was your computer, but they were waiting for you to realize it for yourself. That is when you try to somehow casually turn down the volume, acting as if there was really no big deal about what just happened. I got out of that situation relatively unscathed but the Debbies out there were definitely taking note.

Blocking Out Time

There were certain times when I simply did not want people to schedule meetings. From 9:30 A.M. to 10:30 A.M. Eastern each day, I wanted to be at my desk with access to the markets if need be. The same was true from 3 P.M. to 4 P.M. Eastern. These time periods tend to be the most volatile periods in a market session, and I felt that it was imperative to not have any work distractions during these time periods.

That does not mean I would not do any work during this time, but it did mean that I was paying much less attention to my job responsibilities and more attention to the financial markets when compared to other times throughout the day. Obviously, though, I could not simply send out a mass e-mail to my peers telling them to quit scheduling meetings during those times because that, for sure, would not fly well with others.

Give No Option

So for years, I would block out the 9:30 A.M. to 10:30 A.M. Eastern time block each day, showing it in the same color coding as the meeting color that is used. I would do this as well for the 3 P.M. to 4 P.M. time slot as well. You will want to make sure these are recurring meetings for each day of the week, so you do not have to input the meetings for each new day. After you do it once, you will not have to do it again.

Now, when all those meetings are getting scheduled by the Larrys, Debbies, Edwards, and Garys of the workplace, you have about a 95 percent chance when they are looking at availability among meeting attendees that they will not schedule it during the times that you have blocked out. If they do, there is a good chance that your being there is not a big deal to the meeting organizer; otherwise, why would he schedule it during a time that your calendar shows a meeting conflict?

I always made sure to have these meeting times blocked out, and it always gave me the opportunity to observe the market action when I needed to the most. The times you choose to block off should take both the job responsibilities and your trading strategy into account. It may not be the same hours that I chose, but it should be specific to a time period(s) that you need to see the market based on the trading strategy you are using.

■ Sneaking Out of Meetings

It is not at all uncommon now for meeting participants to be interrupted with phone calls on their cell phone. Unless there is a company policy against this, you can definitely use it to your advantage. Often, I would push a button on my phone that would cause my default ringtone to go off. At first, I would look at my phone to see who was calling me and make it look like I was contemplating whether to take the call. Then I would say in a soft voice to everyone in the conference room, "Excuse me, I'm sorry, I have to take this," as I then proceeded to get out of my chair and head for the door, but before I got to the door, but still within earshot of the meeting participants, I would fire off a stern, "This is Ryan!," which gave the whole delivery a more serious tone that made it sound nothing like a personal call but a something that must be work related.

The humor in it all is that I had no one on the phone, I was just wanting to get out of the meeting so I could enter a trade or get a market update on my existing positions and then get back into the meeting. Of course, once I had the laptop, I could just do it right there in the meeting.

By the way, if you do not have to sit at the meeting table, and there are seats lined up around the perimeter of the conference room that you could take instead, then I highly recommend you do that. It just tends to keep you away from the fray of the meeting, and it is much easier to use your laptop or other personal instruments without drawing much attention to yourself.

Considering Extreme Measures

There was really nothing that I hated more than being in a meeting. I came up with everything I could think of to avoid going to them. The worst was all-day events, where more than once I actually thought about purposefully collapsing on the ground, trying to foam out the mouth, and faking a seizure right there in front of everyone.

It was the surefire way to get out of the boredom that ensnared me. However, the prospect of my being able to stay "in character" if one of my colleagues attempted mouth-to-mouth resuscitation on me was more than I could bear. Also, the thought of being taken to the hospital and being hooked up to an IV and other equipment for a seizure that did not actually happen was a bit of a problem as well, but having to choose between a bed and cable television versus staying in that meeting for a minute longer might have given the slight edge to the fake hospital trip.

Calling In as Much as You Can

With modern technology, one of the best advancements is the ability to call in and share your desktop with others. That means you do not actually have to leave your work area to attend a meeting. That also means regardless of whether you work off of a desktop or laptop, it does not matter because you can call in to your meeting without having to miss a beat in your trading.

Bailing Out

At times I had meetings that were only down the hallway, and I would still call in because I would rather just be relaxed in my own office setting. The only problem was that sometimes I could go a long stretch in a meeting without having to speak, and I would zone out doing something else that had nothing to do with the meeting when suddenly I would hear someone say, "Ryan, would you like to chime in on that?"

The problem then became that I had no idea what they were asking me to "chime in" on because I simply had not been paying a single bit of attention to what was being talked about. Sometimes, I did not even know what the meeting was about. I would just call in for the sake of virtually attending the meeting that did not really matter to begin with. Instead of asking them to repeat the question or dig around for what they wanted an answer for, I simply took the easiest way out.

I hung up the phone!

I would then proceed to call back in, punch in the access code, and then they would hear me come back into the meeting. I would proactively state, "Sorry folks, I got dropped somehow from the meeting. What did I miss?" as if I had no idea I had been asked a question. At this point, they would provide the background and repeat the question, and then I could actually tell them what they wanted to know, without having to look like a moron for never having listened at all to the meeting.

Avoid the Screen Share

A final piece of advice in regard to meetings concerns screen sharing. Do not offer to share your screen unless you are put in a corner with no possible way out. There is so much that can go wrong by doing this. Your trading platform sometimes will flash messages on your screen, make noises, or pop up an alert on your e-mail software letting you know that you have been stopped out of a position. The last thing you want to do is allow people to have familiarity with your trading habits.

On one such occasion I was asked to host the meeting remotely with all the other participants. There were about 30 people in total, with about 15 of them being clients of ours. I had a meeting agenda that I was streaming for everyone to see. All was going well, until I started to do basically what I do at every meeting—zone out. I was not paying attention to anything that was being said, and since we were not in a local meeting room, there really was not any opportunity to start seizing in order to get out of the meeting.

Instead, I started looking at some of my favorite web sites, like ESPN, to see how my local Orlando Magic did the night before and to get caught up on some box scores. Then, all of a sudden, an Edward on the conference call caught my attention when he said my name:

"Ryan, who won the Magic game last night," he asked.

Puzzled, I said, "I dunno, why?"

He sarcastically replied with, "I figured you'd know since you are on ESPN right now."

Then I realized how big an idiot I was. I became so bored in the meeting that I started surfing the Internet in front of 30 individuals. Thankfully, it was not my trading account that they were being introduced to, and just a sports site instead.

■ How to Trade When Traveling

There were times at my job when I would travel up to 75 percent of the time. It was definitely a great way to get out of the office, although when budgets started getting tight, the boss man would try and have me fly out on my weekends. That was one area where I simply refused. They would want me to leave on a Sunday evening, fly for six hours, check into the hotel, meet with another company all day long the next day, and then catch the red-eye that night back home.

Honestly, that has to be one of the most inconsiderate requests to make of an employee. We work five days a week, then you want to take one of my only two days off and dedicate it to flying so that I do not spend any of my work time actually sitting on an airplane. Those who were paid as hourly employees were not even paid for flying during their off time.

You Can Still Trade

When it comes to flying and traveling in general, there is no reason why you cannot still carry long or short positions. The only thing is that you have to be willing to not have as much access to your stocks while you are traveling. That means you are using hard stops on all your trades—no questions asked. When you are traveling, you are not as likely to have access to your positions unless you are on layover or are on one of those planes that have wireless connectivity. Consequently, the stocks you were trading might have had a negative press release or maybe even a surprise earnings announcement causing the stock to drop a considerable amount. In this case, you will be very thankful that you had a stop loss in place to make sure that you got out at your exit price.

West Coast Trading Another benefit, as mentioned in earlier chapters, is that if you live on the East Coast of the United States, the further west you fly, the more hours you will have to be an active market participant in the mornings before you would typically have to start working.

I always enjoyed flying out to Oregon and California because the market opened up much earlier in the morning when I was in their time zone. So there were plenty of opportunities, depending on the location, that allowed me to benefit from the time change and actually experience brief moments of being completely focused on the markets without the encumbering job requirements.

If you are not a fan of flying during market hours because you do not want to be disconnected from your existing positions, then consider flying during non–market hours when you are worried about your current positions. This is much easier to do living closer to the West Coast than on the East, as the market closes earlier and allows for you to still travel during business hours.

However, on the East Coast, this is much more difficult to accomplish unless you want to fly in the evening. I was never a big fan of this because I'd rather be settling into my hotel at night, instead of having my private areas groped by the TSA at the security lines.

Adding New Positions Prior to Travel

I do not necessarily think that this needs to be etched in stone, but traveling with open positions in the market does carry an additional level of risk simply because you may not always be able to have access to the financial markets when they are being actively trading, and if I had to vote one way or the other, I would vote against adding new positions right before you leave on a business trip.

With your existing positions, you already have an idea for their tendencies and how they are likely to act. If it is a stock that you are not as familiar with, there is a level of "unknown" that you are playing with, not only with the individual stock but the fact that you are adding risk to your portfolio with more capital committed. If you can sell out of a stock for reasons that make sense to your style of trading, then it might not be a bad idea to do so, considering it will lessen your risk exposure to your capital while you are unable to be at the helm.

Using the Travel Time

I also strongly encourage traders, when traveling, to use their time at night in the hotels to their benefit. If you have a family back at home, sometimes the evenings can be a difficult time to get a lot of research and studying done on the market. However, when traveling, often you are holed up in your hotel with nothing much to do. Use that time to read, research, and strategize.

One time I went on a business trip to New Jersey. We got in pretty late that night (sometimes you do not have an option about when you can travel when flights get delayed). We found the only place that looked like it would satisfy our appetite. In this case, it was Red Lobster, and I am a huge fan of their cheese biscuits. I am pretty sure they were running their all-you-can-eat shrimp deal that night, and to say the least, there must have been a shrimp that was not quite agreeable with my stomach, because the rest of the night I spent bear-hugging the bathroom toilet in my hotel room.

I did not get much sleep at all, and when the sun rose and I met up with the team, they asked me what happened. They told me to stay back (out of fear that it was some kind of shrimp virus that they might all catch), and I offered no resistance.

I actually did not feel all that bad, since by then I had the food out of my system. Later that morning I started feeling much better, and it gave me an entire day to trade the markets and enjoy some time doing extra research, creating new scans, and even some reading to myself. I think it was the best day I ever had on the job. In fact, I was tempted to figure out how I could get food poisoned every time I traveled if it meant I could hang out in the hotel all day.

Using Your Workload to Your Trading Benefit

Rule of thumb: Never tell the boss man you have nothing to do—particularly if you are bent on becoming a full-time trader. This can kill you, not literally, but certainly for trading successfully. Always do what they ask you to do, but in my opinion, it is the boss man's job to determine the workload, and it is your job to get it done as fast as you can, so you can focus your energies on more important matters.

Here's what happens when you ignore my advice: The boss man will look at everyone else's workloads and try to find someone who is overworked and then offload some of their assignments onto you. This person is now vested in your success because they already have invested to some extent their own time and energy in the project that you are being given. So they will likely be a bit of a micromanager on how well you handle everything and carry out your assignments. You do not need this. What is even worse is when your own responsibilities that were idle at the time kick back up, and you are left doing someone else's work that the boss man assigned, while also trying to make sure the assignments you had previously on the job do not get neglected either. It is really a no-win situation.

A "Debbie" in the Making

I unwillingly fell into this situation once, when sources unbeknownst to me filled in the boss man that I did not have much of a workload. My coworker Tess was loaded to the gills, but she was also a "Debbie" in her approach to work. I was not very giddy about wanting to help her out, but I got assigned some of her work nonetheless. I kid you not, she would call me in the double digits each day asking for a status update. I took the following approaches with her:

- Drive her nuts by acting like I was oblivious to what she was wanting me to do.
- Pick up the phone when she called and immediately hang it up loudly enough she could hear the clicking noise definitively and know that it was intentional.

Or my personal favorite:

- Answer all her questions nicely and professionally, but constantly talking to her with the phone receiver cord being unplugged and plugged in over and over again, so she only catches about every fifth word in our conversation.

Ultimately, this level five clinger who obsessively called me practically every hour on the hour grew so frustrated that she took back the work on her own. I am not saying that is the course of action you want to take. I was on my way out. I knew I did not have much time before I would be giving my resignation, so I took the liberty of going to war with this coworker of mine.

The biggest thing when it comes to taking on other assignments, if you are forced to, is to have an exit plan on how to give it back to the coworker when the other responsibilities that you had start picking back up again; otherwise, you will be forced to kiss your part-time trading opportunities good-bye.

Each coworker is different, and you want to be careful how you deal with them, especially when it interferes with your ability to trade. So keep your cool, and work with them in a way that will not land you in the hot seat.

The best way to deal with coworkers most of the time is with kid gloves and not allowing them to get rattled at you personally so that they have the need to knock you off your seat and into the hot seat with the boss man.

Which brings me to my next chapter . . .

CHAPTER 13

What to Say and Do if Trading Becomes a Distraction

The last thing that you can afford to have happen as a trader is to allow your interest in the financial markets to be known among the colleagues that you work with. Being a distraction is bad—in fact, it is possibly catastrophic. That's right, "catastrophic" to your ability to successfully trade. If the boss man catches wind that even though you are successfully doing your job, you are also indulging yourself in part-time trading, then your trading will be done for. That is, unless he uses logic and reason in his thinking; then he might turn a blind eye since you get your work done and do a good job at it in the process.

However, if you suck at your job, forget about it! And if that is the case, you should not be reading this book in the first place. Instead, you should try to gain some respect for yourself in the workplace, not pick up an additional habit that will give boss man a reason to kick you to the curb. If you are not performing at the level you should be at your job, you can rest assured that the boss man is looking for any reason to lighten the company of the burden you have become to it.

Here's the big reason for your keeping your trading under wraps: Once the boss man realizes you have time to support a part-time trading endeavor, no matter how limited the time is dedicated to the craft, you are at risk of his assuming that you do not have enough work to do. Instead of using rational thinking and cutting you some slack by letting you continue trading as long as you maintain your job responsibilities, he is just going to throw more work on your plate.

In reality, that is one of the more stupid things most of your Edwards, Debbies, and Garys will do. As a manager, you risk threatening a delicate balance. When you have a solid contributor on your team, you do not give him more work just because you think there may be 20 minutes of unused time in his day. No way. If the person is not a problem, you leave him alone. It is like the old saying, "If it's not broken, do not fix it"; the same is true with employees: if an individual is doing some trading on the side while meeting or exceeding expectations on the job, do not go messing with his workload. In doing so, you will only create for yourself a disgruntled employee.

What You Must Avoid at All Costs

When I was working in the cube farm, there was a man working a few stalls to my left. He was not a part-time trader, but he apparently had a penchant for cooking and selling beef jerky. You could hear him throughout the day calling his wife to remind her that she needed to take one batch out of the oven and put another one in. Later in the day, you could hear him talking with people interested in buying his jerky or cold-calling various stores to carry his line. Let's just say everyone knew him and what he was doing. It was not an issue really, until he screwed up with an assignment on his real job.

It was not even that big a deal in terms of what he did wrong, but when you screw up, everyone is looking to cover themselves to make sure the blame does not fall on them. So guess who becomes the easy target? That's right, the guy running the beef jerky business—"Maybe if he wasn't more concerned about double checking the beef jerky temperature he was cooking it at, we would not have forgotten to invoice the customer!" That is a hard one to refute when it is said, and when it comes to his coworkers making sure they come out of the hiccup unscathed and look better in the process despite the problem at hand, you can forget about people not using every piece of leverage they have and putting it on the easiest target and making them the scapegoat in order to save themselves from harm.

How to Deal with Those Who Are Far Too Curious

People will talk and, far worse, people will embellish what they do not know or understand. When you are a part-time trader on the side, your coworkers assume that you are a full-time hedge fund manager who is running a Ponzi scheme at work with company pension funds. That might be extreme, but what I want you to realize, fair or not, is that people will talk about everything they think you might be doing on the job. The details that are fuzzy will just be filled in with whatever makes the gossip that they share the juiciest.

I worked in a lot of different areas and I had the benefit of not having to work with one set of people for too long. One thing that I tried to do, and it may or may not serve you well in your job, is unplug my network cable at night, particularly if I was not going to shut down my computer. The network cable looks like a phone cord, and serves as the connection between your computer and the company's servers.

Most companies will back up their files at night after everyone has gone home. Often, this consumes server resources that they do not want to use when everyone is going to be accessing or on the network (i.e., peak office hours). If you have a coworker that complains about you, they will look at backup files of your computer to see what was on there the day before and to determine whether there is something that is worth taking action on. Personally, I would avoid storing anything on the hard drive that would be related to trading, and most certainly would never store anything on the company's network. But if you are going to put some stuff on the hard drive anyway, you may just want to unplug your network cable prior to leaving each night.

Don't Drop Your Guard

That is far from a foolproof solution, particularly since there is technology out there now, such as the keystroke software, and others where programs on the network will actually take periodic print-screen snapshots of exactly what is on your monitor (it can be every 30 minutes and sometimes as aggressive as every 5 seconds) as it essentially looks through your vantage point in real time. Many times, this software will not get turned on until Human Resources or the boss man has reason to because the amount of storage it would require (even in a small company) would carry a lot of expenses in doing so.

That is why it is so important to remain off the radar because once there is a complaint or a suspicion about your work ethic or that you may be a part-time trader, you are going to be facing some problems, even if it is not warranted. This is also the reason why I did everything I could to be liked by my colleagues—not because I'm a people-pleaser or need to be everyone's friend, but I knew that not making that effort to do so creates the possibility of having enemies at work, and in all honesty, that is the last thing I really wanted for reasons already stated.

Getting Coworkers Off Your Scent

Always act like an idiot when it comes to the stock market. If someone is talking about stocks, the direction the market is going in, or simply something that is about to bait you into the conversation, do not fall for it. That is the beginning of a slippery slope that will lead you to trying to validate your opinion with your own credentials as one who has a heavy involvement in the financial markets. When asked about the market, I would play dumb by saying, "I was always told it was best to buy low and sell high." That way, I did not have to make some comment that made it look like I was from another planet, but also deflecting the conversation by stating one of the most overused trading expressions without giving myself away as so much more than some casual market observer.

Stay Neutral

If worse comes to worst, and the boss man calls you into his office about negative feedback from your coworkers but you know you are doing a good job and not letting others know about your trading, then there should not be any conversations about trading. Be careful, though, about being defensive with the boss. If you know you are in the right, and have the political capital at work to get away with it, then you should be fine.

As a part-time trader aspiring for the full-time life, you are trying to protect the opportunity at a future way of life. Scoring points at work is not what you need to be seeking. Ruffling the feathers of others can only spell trouble for you down the road when someone decides to get back at you for the smallest of slip-ups. The one thing you do not want to have happen is for your trading and the ability to do it successfully to become compromised and ultimately done away with.

When Trouble Occurs

I had one such run-in once with a woman we will call Debbie Douchay. This was my one moment in Corporate America that taught me to hate everything about working in a competitively charged working environment, where they promote the dog-eat-dog mentality in a far-too-aggressive manner. Do not get me wrong, I am capitalist as it gets; otherwise, I would be writing this book for free (which obviously I am not doing), and of all things I would not have my greatest passion in the smallest of details that makes Wall Street tick.

Matters Become Out of Control The events that transpired put me over the edge. I doubled down on my commitment to becoming the full-time trader and succeeding as the part-time trader in the process. Essentially, the boss man that I was working for was one of those eight bosses that I tried not to purposefully upset. She was so wicked that she made Somalian pirates look like Boy Scout troop leaders.

Apart from being unethical to the core and consistently asking me to fudge numbers and break company policy that would lead to my immediate dismissal, she also thought that I was somehow her secretary that would go fetch her coffee and run her personal errands. That just was not going to jive well for me. We were on a business trip, and I remember in front of customers and coworkers alike Douchay criticized my note-taking at the meeting simply because she could not understand my personal notes, even though I would later transcribe and print them out as meeting minutes for others to read. When negotiating price with a long-time customer of ours, she negotiated a deal that ruined a decade-old relationship with one of our best customers. This was unprecedented, and when I raised an objection to the long-standing agreement she was forcing both sides to work outside of, she ferociously objected to what I had to say, and despite my being the only person who could commit the corporation to an agreement, she went over my head and negotiated without my being present.

Bad Turns Worse

When we got back to the home base, I was confronted with the demand to take part in additional behavior that was also wrong. I refused to do so. As a result, she took action against me, complaining to the boss man's boss man that she wanted me kicked off the job. Because she was poker buddies with this person, her wish was granted. The grim reality of being reassigned to a different project due to "behavior that was detrimental to the team" made it to where any possibility of a pay raise or promotion the following year was impossible.

I provided all the evidence and e-mails showing how Douchay was exercising a personal vendetta against me. Even her personal and unethical behavior was brought to light. I was told that while I was right in what I did, Douchay was wrong, and I had no business being kicked off the program, but they refused to take action because I was too low on the totem pole, and Douchay's poker buddy had far too much power to risk their own credibility for my sake. So I became the sacrificial lamb.

At the end of the day, Douchay survived and continued to do what she was doing and wrecking other careers to cover up her own shortcomings. While none of what I have written here has much to do with trading on the surface, there are some important lessons that you can learn at my expense.

Soon thereafter, a number of individuals wanted me to sign a petition involving nearly 90 percent of the people working under Douchay and submit it to Human Resources for her unethical behavior. Personally, I would have loved to do it, but that was not my objective in my place of employment. My objective was to remain employed and perform my job at an acceptable level, while growing my part-time trading endeavor into an eventual full-time position one day.

Getting caught up with Human Resources could lead to far greater problems that were not in my "strategic guide plan" for eventually ditching this place one day. As a result, I declined to take action and let them find someone else to lead the charge. Unfortunately, nobody else wanted to take the reins either, and Douchay got away with everything that she had done.

Stay the Course

As I've mentioned time and time again, my objective was to stay below the corporate radar. I did not want to be "known." In fact, the fewer people that knew my name, the better. If I took Douchay to Human Resources, who knows, it could have turned on me, and I might have eventually been the one on the hot seat for reasons beyond my control. As a result, I declined to retribution, despite badly wanting it. The one radar you definitely want to avoid being on at all costs is Human Resources'. They have the tools and means to do what they want, and the fewer number of people in that organization that knew my name, the better it was for my future aspirations.

That common saying of "stay the course" could not have rung more true in this situation. Revenge was the natural reaction for me to rectify a wrong that had been done. I wanted justice, and I wanted to clear my name and make sure somebody paid for trying to throw me under the bus in the process. However, looking back years later, would I be where I am at today, free from the responsibilities of Corporate America and instead doing what I love most? Perhaps not.

Leading a coup d'etat against Douchay could have hampered my ability to trade as a part-timer and ultimately (particularly if she could have turned the tables on me yet again) led to my dismissal or spending a longer time on the job than what I had originally expected. When you start taking those corporate actions against another employee who has some sway and pull, you never know for sure what the outcome is going to be, and sometimes that outcome can come with devastating consequences. When that happens, Douchay would just win again, and at the expense of my being able to trade part-time.

Could Have Been Worse

What would have happened if Douchay knew that I was part-time trading as well? Even though my trading did not inhibit my performance on the job, it still would have been thrown into the mix as part of the problem, and, unfortunately, management would have acted on that and shut down my ability to trade part-time and possibly my job as well. There was no point during my time in Corporate America where I was more thrilled that I had kept all my trading endeavors to myself over all those years.

The boss man loves to have a possible smoking gun to pin the blame on. If my performance was really as bad as it was said by Douchay (and no one actually believed it was), then it would have been blamed directly on my trading. That is why I was so steadfast and remaining private about all of my trading activities on the job. Otherwise, my trading would have been shut down.

I Could Have Done Better

I also made a mistake during this time as well, by making an enemy out of a person who could have created far worse problems for me. Sure, the unethical behavior I did not have to sign up for, but I could have easily said, "Sure I'll do it; right after my organizational boss man approves the action." She would have been less likely to push the request had I tried to "innocently" involve my other boss man (Douchay was the project manager). Or, even better, ask for the request in an e-mail and then forward it to the boss man for approval. Another attitude I should have had was a bit more humility. What is the harm in grabbing one's coffee, though I had no reason to do so on the surface? I definitely would have looked like I was some kind of corporate tool that would do anything and everything requested by the powers that be.

Stay "Cool" Remember *Cool Hand Luke* after he had been captured following multiple escape attempts. They beat him to a pulp, and he started to cower down to the prison guards who ran the show, and submit to their every request. His inmates and buddies abandoned him, flicked burned-out cigarettes on him, and turned their backs on him in time of need. When he was busy doing roadwork with the rest of the crew, he would fetch the water from one truck, the gun from another and anything else, including when Boss Godfrey shot with his rifle the turtle in a nearby pond.

The inmates showed disdain, but all the while he was running around and doing what Boss Godfrey asked him to do, he was fetching the keys out of all the vehicles as well, so that he could eventually make his escape in the truck when asked to throw the dead turtle in the back of it. He would drive off leaving the guards without any way to pursue him and all his inmates cheering him on as they regained their long-lost pride in Luke.

Likewise, you have to be somewhat as cunning as well in your behaviors. I definitely was not as sly as I should have been when it came to Douchay, and it could have cost me big time as well. Cool Hand Luke understood what he wanted to eventually do: leave the prison forever under the newfound guise of trust that the security had placed upon him, only to break free and never have to wear those chains again.

Having to do what you ultimately do not want to do does not mean that you are flushing your dignity down the toilet, though it will seem that way to those around you, but you are giving yourself every opportunity to succeed as a part-time trader and ultimately break free of those corporate chains and drive off to your career as a full-time trader.

When Boss-Man Comes A-knockin'

We have all had those awkward and uncomfortable meetings with the boss man. Often, we build up the horror of them more in our heads than what actually becomes reality. I always tended to assume the worst myself. Perhaps as a trader that is why I am constantly focused on the risk side of the trade rather than becoming enamored with the profits that I might be collecting on it.

Should you be confronted by the boss man about the trading activity, I would not try to not hide it. Once you are being asked, it is a near certainty that they know you are a trader. That is not necessarily a bad thing. I actually had the boss man ask me for my opinion on nearly every trade he made. Luckily, he left the company before that could actually blow up in my face (very early on in my career). More times than not, though, they are going to want to address a problem at hand, not immerse themselves in it. I would never recommend lying to your boss or telling him something that is not true. That, my friend, will only get you into trouble. Instead, be honest. Let the boss man know that you are fascinated by the markets and that you like to keep up with it during the day, just as a news junkie likes to remain abreast of the latest news events and developments.

Problems with Day Trading

The reason I say that day trading is so difficult to accomplish on the job is that it requires the constant monitoring of the financial markets and combining that with the need to do a good job with the workload the boss man has assigned to you. That means either you will not be able to successfully trade or you will find yourself neglecting the work that should still be your first priority. So when you find yourself in the boss man's office, you do not want to be confronted with the reality that you have to admit that you have been day trading throughout the day because the odds are that you are in the boss man's office in the first place because you neglected your job in some form or manner.

I did not day trade outside of the stories I have already told you about. Instead, I was a swing trader. I found that this particular approach to the markets freed me up dramatically to meet expectations that were placed on me by the boss man, all the while being able to follow the markets, but without having to be concerned with every tick and movement that the market made.

In fact, I found that the markets as a part-time swing trader on the job eliminated a lot of the emotional pitfalls that comes with trading. I could not watch the market all the time, so I was able to avoid being shaken out of positions due to an emotional response to the markets and instead allowed my hard stop losses that I had already set to work their magic. This was very helpful early on in my development because it is easy to see typical market spasms that run against a position and believe the position needs to be closed out to avoid further losses, even before the position gets stopped out.

Swing Trading to the Outside Person

Being a swing trader in the boss man's office then becomes much more explainable than if you were running a hedge fund, day trading, scalping, or some sophisticated all-consuming trading strategy. That is why planning your strategy around your workload is imperative. If you are a person who is house-sitting for a job, or a security guard monitoring a car garage, or a fireman on call until the next emergency strikes, or something similar, then you can be a day trader. Other jobs, though, where you have a daily workload and meetings and other matters that must be attended to will not give you the same flexibility, and as a result, you need to make sure that any trading strategy you adopt is conducive to your work schedule.

Plenty of people trade while on the job, and there is a good chance that the boss man does some trading of his own. It is just that the objective that he is trading under is not to become a full-time trader and rid himself of his employer. The difference is that his passions are with his regular daytime job. For the part-time trader like me, it was with the financial markets, with my job simply being a means to an end. The passion and approach were at opposite ends of the spectrum, but when you are confronted by the boss man, it does not require you to reveal your degree of loyalty to your trading versus your job. That is internal to you, and nothing that needs to be revealed to the powers that be about that.

When asked, then, explain your trading in a way that eliminates any revelation about your passion for the true career path you are on and instead focus on the basics of what you do.

I have talked about this constantly throughout the book—don't do your research when you are on the job. Instead, the research should be done the morning of or the night before. As a swing trader, you are not averaging tons of trades each day, so you are likely only doing a few trades each market session, and the time component to enter those orders is marginal. Of course, you are going to keep track of how those positions do throughout the day, but not via nonstop monitoring. Assuming that you are the employee who gets his work done and still makes his corporate job the priority (when it comes to accomplishing the daily workload), watering down your trading to the bare basics of how you explain it to the boss man and what it really is, means that it probably won't differ much from the time and effort a lot individuals spend watching the financial markets during the day. The only difference will be your passion and devotion to the markets, which is no one's business but your own.

More of My Personal Tricks of the Trade

There is a verse in the Bible, from Matthew 10:16, that says "… to be wise as serpents and innocent as doves." My goal in writing this book is to help those who want to be a part-time trader while having a completely different job that they need, and furthermore helping you set yourself on the path to becoming a full-time trader one day. Whether you hope to achieve the latter or are content in remaining in the former, this book was written for you. I have shared my successes and failures and have done everything I can to open up to you as a trader and individual who lamented my job: some because of my own doing, and others because of the simple nature of what it means to work with others in a corporate setting.

All of these tricks and stories that I have written about were not always as funny when they were actually unfolding, but there are lessons to be learned from them, and all of these tactics that I employed on my job were not done to mislead or cheat the system. Rather, they were done to help me progress in a career aspiration that I had and was unrelated to the job at hand. I did this without being a malcontent at work or not performing at the level that was expected of me.

The concept of working in Corporate America is not the enemy. But there is a problem, and that arises from the individuals with whom we work. You see, we all have our own downfalls, pitfalls, and letdowns that we all have to deal with and improve on. When you introduce into your life the idea of making additional money by trading the financial markets while you are working, people are going to become jealous and envy any success that you might experience if you let them in on your supposed-to-be secret endeavor.

Image and Performance

Unfortunately, the "image is everything" phrase carries a lot of weight in the workplace, and my approach to how I worked and the steps that I took to preserve the perception that the boss man and coworkers held of me was paramount to my trading success. I never changed as an employee. No matter which company I worked for, or the person who oversaw my progress, my performance never changed, and my ability to achieve the goals that were set out for me to attain were never compromised. I was sold out to part-time trading, but I viewed my responsibilities as an employee as part of my ability to trade successfully. Without a paying job, I could not have been a successful part-time trader, and without part-time trading while on the job, I could have only attained the status of full-time paper trader, because I would not have had the necessary capital requirements to do it on my own.

Everything Has to Align Together

I knew that I could do well on the job. I was in a world where most were not as technically savvy on the computer as I was, and what some could do in 3 hours, I could oftentimes finish in 30 minutes. Not because I was smarter, but I was more tactical and knew how to get the job done in a way that was easier. This would afford me a lot of extra time to follow the markets when I wanted or needed to. Unfortunately, when dealing with others on the job, they are not going to look at the actual facts. They are going to assume that if you are successful as a part-time trader, you will be a horrible employee. While that might be true for some, it is not an absolute that can be applied across the board. Being a solid contributor was not the obstacle for me. It was making sure that the image that I projected to everyone matched the expectations that I was performing at.

My reason for doing so was to keep trading out of the discussion: to eliminate the need or provide a reason for being suspicious about me.

Individuals and boss men alike can get caught up in the notion that regardless of their actual performance, the illusion or image that is being projected to others is unacceptable and changes have to be made. That is not something you want to have happen to you. The key is to remain in control of your own domain, to project the image of the successful and ideal employee, performing at the acceptable level of work required of you, all the while being a part-time trader who can navigate the financial markets at the same time.

Learning to Do Two Things at Once

I'm not going to tell you that balancing the workload the boss man gives you with trading part-time will be an easy endeavor. It is very difficult, and often you will be forced to choose between the two. I am not very good at doing two things at once; in fact, I do not even like to multitask when it comes to such simple things as eating. I usually only eat one type of food on my plate before moving on to the next food. Typically, I start with the food that I like the most, then I move on to the next best food, and then finally the last thing I eat will be what I dislike the most (and it's usually cold by the time I start on it). I am not even that big a fan of casseroles because I like to have my food separated and not touching one another. Sort of like how McDonald's gives you a paper-wrapped cheeseburger, a drink, and an order of fries in a box. That is how I like my food. I need to have something here, here, and here.

I'll Second That

Unfortunately, when it comes to trading, I cannot do that. One of my best acquisitions while I was working the paper-pushing job was getting a second monitor. I got the monitor simply by strolling through an abandoned office area and noticing that there was a monitor sitting on one of the desks collecting dust. There was no computer to which it was attached, so I took it and brought it back to my office. It cannot be considered stealing when all I did was relocate the monitor to a different desk within the same building.

Let the boss man know that by having an additional monitor, you will become more efficient in your work, which is 100 percent true. By having that second monitor, I was able to better balance that relationship between trading and job responsibilities (which, of course, made me more efficient!).

Don't Do Research at Work

While there is this idea that you know what you are likely to be confronted with when you arrive at work, we all know that rarely does a day on the job go according to plan. Instead, you are thrown curve balls that you were not expecting to have, and you have to adjust accordingly. Trying to research at work is far too time consuming to do before the market opens, and if you think you can do so uninterrupted, the likelihood is a farce. Leave the research for at home, have it done by the time you arrive, and simply focus on implementing the plan you have already laid out for yourself.

Once you have a position that is on, you cannot simply sit there and watch every tick at the expense of what you should be doing. Most traders, full-time and part-time alike, get themselves into trouble when they start watching the markets too closely. When you have your stop-loss in, let your analysis and studies do their work. Of course, there are times when you should adjust your stops to take advantage of market situations, and you should no doubt be cognizant of what the market is doing throughout the day if that is possible. But do not get absorbed at the expense of everything else that you should be tending to.

■ Network Tricks

Most companies have a protected network, but what they also provide guests access to the network without requiring login and user password. When I was on the job, unless I needed to be logged in to access the network, I did all my work through the guest portal. Since I saved everything on my computer and would always wait until an assignment was completed before uploading my documents to the server, I would log on through the guest network and stay there throughout the day.

Be Our Guest

Guest networks give you a little bit more anonymity (let's face it, nothing on the Internet is anonymous) as your information technology (IT) group is less likely to monitor this part of the network's activity, since it is open access to anyone and everyone. Anyone could be using it—from the person in the parking lot that is just looking for quick access to some free Wi-Fi, to the person waiting in the lobby. Guest networks are much more difficult to track and often times overlooked, which is why it is so hard to monitor or even spot if an employee is on it. That is why I chose to connect to the guest portal once I made sure I did not need to always access the company server.

In those cases where I did need access, I would simply discontinue any web sites that were not needed for me to function in my job, and then switch to the employee side of the network. This would provide me access to the servers and any documents that I needed or wanted to upload. In doing this, I was able to curb my exposure to corporate monitoring, and while nothing in the world of IT is failsafe, you can create favorable odds for yourself of being able to trade in an uninterrupted manner.

Bandwidth Red Flags

When it comes to bandwidth, you must be careful about how much you use of it. Streaming real-time quotes, charts, and Bloomberg television on your desktop could easily lead to some flags being raised. In doing so, you are consuming far more bandwidth that you should be and much more than the average employee, and frankly that causes you to stick out like a sore thumb.

If everyone else is consuming a half megabyte per second and you are consuming five megabytes per second, well then you can be sure that someone in IT will notice this and look into why you are having to consume so much bandwidth while on the job. When they see what you are doing and the applications you are running, it will not matter how much you are accomplishing at work; instead, they will go into regulation and assumption mode and make your life very difficult.

Instead, use applications that will not consume as much bandwidth and, as I have said throughout the book, ones that will help you stay off the radar. Use static web sites that do not stream real-time quotes. There may be times where in order to get into a position you will need live streaming quotes. If you do, I would limit it greatly, and simply do so to get in or out of a position as necessary. Opt for those sites that provide a static quote and require refreshing to get a new quote. By doing so, you will limit how much you watch the markets, thereby preventing you from micromanaging your positions like a "Debbie" while also trying to accomplish the day's work.

Rely on Handheld Technologies for Streaming If you are going to want access to your brokerage platform's real-time streaming or other sophisticated tools, get an unlimited data plan and use your tablet or smartphone for doing that. Buy yourself a portable stand for it, and you will be able to prop it right up there with your monitors and in the process increase your workplace efficiency.

■ Scaling In and Out of Positions

Ultimately, how you get in and out of positions is up to you as well as how you decide to trade. When I am asked how I enter in a stock, I tell them that I get in all at once. One price, one order. When it comes to getting out of a stock, very rarely will I scale out of a position. Instead, it is just like the entry where my exit price consists of only one lot transaction. When I made the transition into the full-time trading career, I kept to this practice. It keeps everything simple and less discretionary, and when I was part of the corporate scene, it gave me all the ability to trade in a manner that met my work schedule and demands of the job.

If you can manage to scale in and out of positions while on the job, that is great, but make sure that you are doing it because it suits your personality and trading profile as well. A lot of traders use scaling methods because they think it helps to limit risk and allows them to get out closer to the top of a move. In essence, it is kind of like having a second chance at getting in and out of a trade.

I actually disagree with this concept, though. Unless you can systematically do this using exact percentages and prices that show doing so provides a noteworthy difference in your trading results through years of back-testing, I would stick to trading entries and exits that consist of one transaction for each of them.

A Simple Breakdown

Here's the reason behind doing this. Say you are trying to stage your entry into a position, and you are going to break up the capital that you want to commit to a trade in quarters. For the sake of simplicity, let's say that you want to get in initially at $10 per share. If the stock goes to $10.10, you will buy again and subsequently at $10.20 and $10.30 as well. The belief is that if you get stopped out, you only get stopped out of a quarter of a position. But actually, the possibility exists that a stock could hit $10.30 and reverse course and you get stopped out instead losing the profits that you had, and taking a much larger loss than had you simply got in with a full position at $10.

If the stock is profitable, and you sell out at $10.50 with the average fill price of all four stages of $10.15, then instead of making 5 percent on the trade, you are left instead with just a gain of 3.4 percent.

Scaling Out of Profits That is assuming as well that you are not staging out of your position. Let's say that you get out of your first quarter position at $10.50 hoping it will go higher. Instead it retracts. Your next quarter position is at $10.40, then $10.30 and then you close out the position at $10.20. Sadly, that solid swing trade has been reduced to a 1.9 percent gain. Throw in commission costs—eight of them in total—and you probably have a trade where you may actually have taken a loss overall on it. Had you got ten in all at $10 and gotten out at $10.50 like you could have, you would walk away with less in commission costs and a 5 percent gain on the trade itself.

On the flip side, let's say you scaled out at $10.50, but benefited from an additional upside move by getting out at $10.60, $10.70, and finally at $10.80. Your exit price was at $10.65. With your average entry still at $10.15, you still make less at a 4.9 percent gain, plus six additional trades that had to be made because you chose to scale in and out.

Scaling Long in a Falling Stock That is not the only way to scale in and out, obviously, but if you choose to get in as the price moves against you with the belief that your average price will be less, you will find that your best trades will very rarely be on full positions, and every stock you get stopped out on will come with increased commissions and at full positions. The reason I say that is that your best trades will typically do their best right out of the gates. The longer a trade drifts below your entry price, the less likely it will be successful.

My best trades always tend to do what they are supposed to do in quick order. Stocks that languish are not worth trading, and when you scale into those positions, you will find on the whole that your positions and the capital that you commit will be toward those stocks that languish or, even worse, fail, while your best stocks will give you only limited exposure to their potential gains.

The math just does not support scaling in and out. Like I said, unless you can systematically prove that your trading strategy will benefit you in doing so, and is provable over, at least, the past five years, there is no reason to do so. Besides, trying to work and trade successfully by doubling, tripling, or even quintupling the number of trades you place can create some major headaches for you when it comes to trading successfully.

■ Don't Be Too Social

One thing I learned early on is to avoid meaningless interaction with others as much as possible. There are plenty of people out there that would chomp at the bit to spill the beans on a part-time trader while they undoubtedly spend 10 times the amount of time at the water cooler, coffee maker, and everyone's office trying to get their fill of the latest workplace gossip. Even worse are the chronic smokers who believe it is their constitutional right to take a smoke break every 15 minutes while the company pays them to do otherwise. While I would not consider myself one who entertained himself in the affairs of others, I could get bored enough with my job where it would be quite easy to shoot the breeze with some of the folks around the office as well.

No Seats Here

One step that I took about halfway through my corporate career was to eliminate any and all chairs except for my own in the office. When you have chairs in your office, it leads to people putting their butts in them. And most people in the office keep their butts staked in that chair until it seems fitting for them to get up and leave. I did not like office confrontation, and asking someone to leave would be more harmful (think creating enemies) than just letting them hang around for five minutes . . . or two hours. Also, I might miss a trade that I would have liked to take because someone came in and jimmied themselves into my chair. So I got rid of them. Every last one of them were taken out. If someone wanted to come in and chit-chat, we would just have to see how long they could last standing up.

No Snacks, Either

Another easy mistake to make is putting a snack on your work desk. You are just inviting anyone and everyone that gets the munchies to come in. I used to constantly have snacks in my office and never realized how much that interrupted my ability to trade. M&Ms were pretty bad, particularly those with the peanuts inside of them, especially if there was a pregnant lady in the office, God bless her, because she would get chocolate cravings that could wipe out a one-pound bag in the blink of an eye, and there is no way I am going to get in the way of a hormonal pregnant woman and her M&Ms.

But there is nothing worse than placing a bowl of pistachios out there for people to snack on. I love pistachios, but that almost undid me as a trader. It does not matter if you have chairs in the office or not, these guys—and, yes, most of them were guys—would come in there like it was the place to be on the 15-minute break and start chomping away at the pistachios. They did not want to take too many at a time; instead, they would just stand there and reach into the bowl repeatedly for more. Besides, my trash can was right there by my desk, so when they got the nut out of the shell, they had to dispose of the rest somewhere. Consequently, these people never left, and I would have to engage in meaningless conversations with them as well—because who eats pistachios without shooting the breeze with your coworker? No one eats pistachios with others in silence, and neither will your coworkers.

Spread the Papers

For some, having to worry about the chairs in the office is not a problem simply because they are stationed in a cubicle. But au contraire! You see, having the cubicle makes you even more vulnerable because, if you have any desk space, and typically you have much more desk space in cubicles, you end up having the guy with the 1980s retro mustache with thick-rimmed glasses coming in with his morning coffee that is half spilling over, only to place his derriere on your desktop spewing nonsense as he tries to tell you the latest corporate developments and intimate details about his job as if you were really interested in knowing anything about it.

The best way to avoid this scenario is to spread stacks of papers or folders across your desk. They will not move the papers to make room for themselves out of fear of messing something up that is important. So once again it comes down to how long they want to place their left hand on top of your cubicle wall to support their weight as they lean into it. At least in the office, you could either shut the door, which blatantly told people to stay out (unfortunately most organizations frown on that behavior, assuming you are up to no good and want no one to see what you are doing), or you could do what I did and just leave the door about a third of the way open so it allows people to come in if they really have to but sort of signaling to them that you have better things you would rather be doing than talking to them. In order to come in, they would have to knock on the door and then push it open, and for some people the psychology of the "one-third door open" maneuver is enough to keep the pesky guests out. In the cubicles, though, you are very susceptible to foreign intruders. Your surest way is to be bold enough to simply tell them you must get back to work. Hopefully, that person will get the message and visit you less frequently and not stay as long next time.

Another way around the all-too-frequent visitor is to have a nearby employee call your office. Each time he starts talking to you, you can politely tell him you have to take the call.

■ It Is a Tricky Way of Life

No one said trading while holding down a full-time job would be easy. It definitely is not. I did not have a guide for doing it, and instead I had to rely on a lot of trial and error. Now you have the one and only authority on part-time trading and how you can do it successfully. Understandably, not every situation is the same, and everything that worked for me will not work for you, and you will want to make sure that you recognize this and modify my strategies to suit your own workplace.

There will be new strategies that you come across, and I would love to hear about them at SharePlanner.com. Just shoot me an e-mail on our "Contact Us" page, and I'll be sure to read and respond to any insights you provide. My biggest hope is that you take what I have written and can find that hope that helps pave the way into full-time trading through successful part-time trading. It takes a lot of discipline, not just with the trading, but also managing a demanding job where everyone holds high and sometimes unreasonable expectations for your work performance.

If it comes down to it, sabotage the trade before you sabotage your job, and always make sure you are not trading so big, with positions that are too large, that you cannot focus on the work at hand. Anxiety from trading is real, and for traders it can be debilitating. When you are trying to manage a job at the same time, it can ruin your reputation and the credibility you have as a contributing member to your organization. Large sums of money, particularly money that you need in the short term, is something that you cannot afford to trade with. When the drawdowns happen (and they will happen), the realization of large sums of capital will paralyze your thinking and you will be far too susceptible to suddenly showing up on the corporate radar when your job starts to become affected by it. You will start watching market action far too closely, spending too much time trying to change what you likely cannot undo, and in the process forgetting about the fact that you ever had a job you were supposed to attend to.

Trade within your means, take what the market can give you, stop watching the dollars, and most importantly make sure that trading successfully also includes successfully managing your job as well.

CHAPTER 15

Take This Job and Shove It

I came to have such a deep disdain for the job that I held that I had imagined the day when I would walk in to the office and give the boss man my two-week notice, and then walk out in a blaze of glory. I would come in with one of those 1980s' boom boxes mounted on my left shoulder with Johnny Paycheck's classic *Take This Job and Shove It* blaring so loudly that everyone would be able to hear it.

I would walk in and slap my resignation on the desk of the boss man and utter a Jim Cramer–like expression such as "Booyah Skeedaddy!" The buildup in my mind created a far more anticlimactic reality when that day finally arrived.

■ How Did I Know It Was Time?

Coming to a final decision was not something that happened overnight—not by a long shot. It was more or less a process where if I was a pot of water on the stovetop, the temperature kept rising and rising to where I started boiling over. This is the point where the choice became more out of necessity and not out of a sudden revelation that came to me. The realization of my future as a full-time trader had dawned.

I Had Arrived

I had a lot of self-doubt to deal with as well. I was not sure if I could make it as a full-time trader or whether I would generate the necessary income that I set out to achieve. Having a paycheck that consistently comes in on the first and fifteenth of every month systematically is something that I have very much grown to appreciate since leaving the workforce. While I have no desire to ever go back and work for someone else, there have been weeks in my own trading where I wish that regular paycheck would reactivate itself.

My trading got to a point to where I could not just trade as a part-time trader. As a caterpillar transforms into a butterfly, I had transformed as well, to where suddenly, as the means was there to quit my job, my skill level and educational experience over many years of trading in the markets basically spoke for itself that I was ready for primetime trading.

A lot of people thought I had lost my mind, as I was doing something that people stopped doing back in the 1990s during the market's tech boom. There were plenty of people who tried to talk me out of my decision, and there is no doubt that it created apprehension leading up to my decision to leave and even after it had been made, when all the events were set in place.

I was going from being a full-time employee in a stable work environment into a very difficult career field that few succeed in. It is one of the most unpredictable professions that one can apply himself to, where no two days are ever alike, and each day offers a new challenge.

■ When I Finally Left

I made sure I would be ready from day one. I did not want to quit my job and suddenly be trying to figure everything out. Instead I built the computer I would trade off of. I did not want to skimp on the most important tool that I would need for my full-time trading career.

Build Your Own

I recommend that you avoid buying an off-the-shelf computer from a store. Those machines typically come loaded to the gills with software that are like sexually transmitted diseases to your computer. They cause all sorts of problems, and once you get them on your computer you never seem to be able to rid yourself of them.

After building my first computer with a lot of help from a close friend, I knew I would never go back to a store-bought one again. Having someone who is skilled in the area of building computers is absolutely necessary. Perhaps your friend in information technology could help you with the task.

But building your own computer gives you a clean and unadulterated platform on which to start your full-time trading career.

Get Some Power Processing power and random access memory (RAM) are two areas that you do not want purchase the minimum of. Look for the best processor out there on the market, preferably an Intel processor if you can. While it varies by computer, I would no doubt get as much RAM as I could. Otherwise, you will find that, as technology improves, your computer will lag more and more with each passing day.

Let's put it this way—my experience with store-bought computers is that they are good for about two years or so and they start breaking down, or they start to malfunction on their own. The ones that I have had custom built are typically cheaper, if you assemble them on your own and buy the parts from a wholesale retailer online. Doing this has resulted in triple the lifetime of my trading computers, and when something breaks down, I can just replace it without having to do anything to the rest of the computer. I have been able to modify my computer as I see fit. At times, it was to put in a new coolant system; another time, I decided I needed to replace the video cards, so that it would put off less heat. I have also recently swapped out my hard drive in favor of a solid-state drive that makes the machine run oh-so-much faster.

Multiple Monitors and Video Cards On the monitor front, you should give strong consideration to having multiple monitors as part of your setup. You don't realize how much you will benefit from having more than one monitor until you actually have more. I know traders who have managed to trade successfully off of a laptop, and kudos to them for achieving that. Multiple monitors will by no means improve your success in the markets, but it will allow you to see more, to view more charts, rather than having to constantly minimize and maximize your screens. I personally have ten monitors stacked five across and two monitors tall. While that might be overdoing it for some, it helps me as well with providing quality content each and every day on SharePlanner.com.

By the way, a word of advice on video cards: stay away from the high-end and high-performance ones if you are going to run multiple monitors. Those cards have a tendency to put out a lot of heat. I replaced my own with some el-cheapo ones and I went from a sweatshop-like environment to a nice and cool office for trading that did not force me to consider trading in my tank-top and skimmies.

Breaking Free

I'll never forget that feeling of walking out the door, not being obligated to return the next day, and literally being off the grid and off the project teams that had controlled my Monday-through-Fridays for well over a decade. The opportunity was finally mine to prove my own worth, not hampered by the constraints of corporate policy, pecking orders, or the office politics that so easily ensnares us all.

I woke up the next day and I went to work—for myself and for my family. It was the first time that my potential had no ceiling to it. What I wanted to become I could make happen with the dedication and hard work that the job would no doubt require of me.

Like any business, I have had my ups and downs, but would not trade the experience for anything, and can only be excited about what the future holds and how it will look 10 years from now. The days are exciting, and the market provides a new story each day for me to trade.

■ Life without Work Benefits

There is plenty to consider when it comes to leaving your job. One aspect I hated leaving was the employee benefits. I had some of the best that you could find, particularly with the health care. Obviously, we had to get our own coverage, and I honestly thought it would cost me an ungodly amount. To my surprise, though, it was not all that bad. A few hundred bucks a month and my family and I were insured. Now that will change as we get older and the susceptibility to different kinds of illnesses becomes far greater. For now, though, if you are still relatively young, you should shop around and find the insurance plan that will benefit you and your family the most.

Then you have the implementation of Obamacare; I have no idea what that is going to do in terms of our ability to acquire quality health insurance on our own and as full-time traders. If history is any indication, massive government programs like Obamacare will result in an equally massive failure and a huge bill for the American taxpayer to foot.

The fact that you are leaving your job does not mean you should not continue contributing to your retirement account. Frankly put, you are not retiring, you are starting a new career in full-time trading, and therefore you need to account for life after your trading days are done and over with. Making sure you have an individual retirement account (IRA) or some other form of savings to support you later in life is absolutely necessary.

Why Did I Do It?

There is no doubt that I could have stayed in the corporate realm and continued with my part-time swing trading. There probably would have been far less stress in many ways. However, the environment that was I was working in was far beyond my tolerance for nonsense, and kick-starting a web site called SharePlanner was another desire of mine that I wanted to be able to partake in. SharePlanner formed out of my experience as a part-time trader and caters to those who are still in that working environment and would like to make their way into the world of full-time trading.

Providing Transparency and Honesty

I have experienced a lot of web sites, and subscribed to many of their newsletters, that simply created the framework that make themselves look like geniuses while covering up their own shortcomings as traders. Others would just flat-out lie about what they had to offer. I would honestly say that 90 percent of the newsletters and subscription-based services offered today in the world of online trading are flat-out garbage and, even if they were offered for free, would not be worth your time or effort. In fact, they would be detrimental to your trading account.

Under this belief, SharePlanner.com was created to show that transparency in individual trades that is lacking everywhere else. I provide my successes, my downfalls, my continued education in the financial markets, and, most important, my lessons learned, and I blog about it multiple times throughout the day, which also includes a daily trading plan that outlines my observations on the market at hand, my strategy for the day going forward, and the positions that I am currently in and how they are performing. This is provided every day, and countless thousands have benefitted from it in the process. Through SharePlanner I wanted to provide for everyone else the exact same information I was providing for myself. Watch lists, trade setups, observations, market analysis, technical analysis, stock screens, and educational lessons and tutorials are all there for you to have for free.

SharePlanner has been blessed as well to have some of the best traders that can articulate their trading and knowledge to their reading base as well. They provide daily trade setups, watch lists, and their own research that they go into each day to trade with. If you are going to trade and equip yourself with all the tools necessary at your disposal, I would highly recommend that you make SharePlanner.com a part of your daily routine.

Premium Services There are other features to further your education, and those I consider to be my "premium" offerings. Despite the fact that it will require some of your own money to be spent on them, they will provide you with an experience at a discounted price that no other site can match. I am consistently in my chat room every day providing my trades in real time (via chat, text, and e-mail alerts), trade alerts, market analysis, and opportunities to trade on. For those looking for more of a long-term solution to managing their IRAs or 401(k)s, I provide a long-term investment system that continuously outperforms the market at large.

There are plenty of educational offerings, such as our online courses and do not forget the free knowledge base of my favorite articles on trading that I have written over the years and will teach you how to trade in different scenarios using strategies of all types.

■ How You Can Know if It Is Time to Leave Your 9-to-5

I once had a conversation with a successful entrepreneur friend of mine, and the question that I asked him was, "When did you know it was time to leave your job?" I was expecting an answer that would reveal the exact time he knew it was right to leave. Instead, he told me, "Ryan, there's never a right time." That answer took me aback. I was hoping to feel inspired by what he would tell me, but instead he told me that the decision to leave the steady paycheck for uncertainty would never come at a perfect time of my choosing. Instead, it will carry risk, and the best thing I could do is prepare myself to the best of my ability and increase my knowledge and understanding of exactly what I was entering into.

To think that I could just seamlessly transition into the world of full-time trading without there being any trials or setback would only be fooling myself.

No Right Time

The notion that you can quantify the perfect time for you to leave will instead leave you constantly waiting without ever actually realizing the opportunity that is yours for the taking. The risks will be there, and if you have taken the shortcuts that I have warned against, then you can expect that to finally catch up with you and possibly affect your chances at living out your dream.

Make no mistake, though—you will want your finances to be in order. At the point where you are contemplating whether you should give the two-week notice, you should have a fair amount of capital lined up and ready to go. This amount of capital should not be suddenly inherited or raised from some outside source, either. Make sure that the money that you are going to trade is an amount of your own that you can live off of from the profits of your success. If it indeed is a lump of cash you have inherited, then you need to get used to trading that kind of capital before you call it quits.

Don't Base It on Inherited Money I have run into far too many traders who have inherited a large sum of cash from a recently deceased relative, and instead of taking the time to learn and gradually build up their comfort level of trading a large portfolio, they put all that money to use right away and try to successfully trade that large sum that they are inherently uncomfortable with.

Build yourself up to that type of capital. The fact that you have the cash on hand does not mean you are ready to trade full-time. The money that you have does not make you a trader; instead, it is the experience, education, and lessons learned from your successes and failures. That alone is what will make you the trader who is ready to take the profession on full-time.

How It Affects Others We cannot make a decision in a vacuum without careful consideration of those that our decision will no doubt affect the most, for better or worse. That is in conjunction with everything you must consider in determining when to make the plunge into full-time trading. You will want love and support from your spouse and even your kids and weigh heavily their opinions on what you should do. Do not think that even in the best of cases you can simply come home from work one day and tell your spouse that you are going to quit your job tomorrow and start trading full-time. Much more times than not, you will be met with heavy resistance.

It is a shocking decision to make. instead, you will want to build up to your final decision with your spouse, and do it only if you have his or her full support and backing. If not, explore the reasons for why, and consider heavily if what you are being told has any truth to it. If so, then consider holding off on those plans to leave. If not, you are in a most desirable position knowing that no matter what happens, your spouse has your back and will support you through good times and bad.

Your children are important, too, with regard to your final decision. If your decision to quit means that your son or daughter has to quit his private school in his junior year and abandon his friends that he has been with since childhood to go to a public school where he knows no one, then give thought to their circumstances as well. It is hard enough to trade as it is; it is even harder if your kids are going to hate you a lifetime for it.

In my senior year in high school, my father was offered a position within his company that would have been his dream job. I was the quarterback of my high school football team, had gone to school with the same kids since I was in first grade, and was at the top of the world in my formative, teenage years. My father understood that uprooting me and relocating me 300 miles south to the beaches of Miami was not something that he felt was in my best interests. It would have been hard on me, and not only did my father understand this, but so did my mother. Consequently, they gave up what would have been the ultimate job on my behalf to ensure that my upbringing was complete and unaffected by their own personal desires. I am beyond grateful for the decision that they made, and no doubt understand that it was a hard one to make, but it was ultimately the right one.

Exactly What Are We Talking About?

In terms of specific amounts of money necessary to become a full-time trader, it varies by the individual and their circumstances. I've seen some individuals quit their jobs and enter the world of full-time trading with only $50,000, and others who waited until they had a $500,000. It all varies by the individual person, his strategy, and his financial needs.

Whatever you think you are capable of making as a trader, you need to cut that in half, heck, and then take that amount and cut it in half again. The greater the expectations that you have for yourself, the harder it will be for you to experience the level of success you aspire to. When you are a full-time trader, it is not about what your percentage return is each year as a trader anymore; instead, it is about feeding your family, providing for them, and doing everything you can to sustain an acceptable income level for your family and you.

The Journey and Not the Destination

The desire to hit the fast-forward button of life and get to the point to where you finally are where you want to be as a trader is understandable. Many times, I found myself nearly scratching at the walls feeling like I was trapped in some kind of asylum at my workplace. Do not let your focus be on your discontent with the job or the fact that you'd rather be trading full-time. You are in an incredible situation, to not have the pressure on your shoulders to perform your trading for a living. The mistakes are easier to recover from, and you have every opportunity to learn from your trades, document your mistakes, and change your strategy, experimenting with various new strategies as you refine, hone, and develop your trading skills.

Just Being a Part-Time Trader If remaining in your job and being a part-time trader into the foreseeable future is what you would rather do instead of aiming for the future career of a full-time trader, then that is terrific. The opportunity is rare, because the work environment continues to become increasingly demanding and difficult to survive in long term as a part-time trader. But if your job gives you the ability to do so, you have an awesome opportunity to have two jobs and do them well, and live a lifestyle that most will never experience.

■ Turning It On

When the "ON" switch is flipped, it is just you and the markets. There is no forgiveness for your mistakes, and the success you experience no one can take from you. Full-time trading allows you to be your own worker and boss man. Not having the latter in my life hovering over me has been great for my own sanity, and though I am my own toughest boss man, I do not have to hate my job or fear what someone else might ask of me next.

Self-Revelation

There is no other profession that will teach you more about yourself, your emotions, and your shortcomings. There is a good chance that until you become a trader, you will never know just how greedy, fearful, and materialistic you are about your own money and the need to make more of it as a result.

In many ways, trading has a refining experience to it because if you do not learn to control these emotions, you become fearful of missing out, greedy in the need to make more than you have, optimistic when you should be pessimistic, and lacking faith when the truth is set before you. Then you will come up short in your aim to become the best trader you can be.

Let's Do It! Saddle up; do the work; plan your trade, trade your plan; learn to trade what you see, not what you think; manage the risk; capture the profits. Avoid the nosy coworker, please the boss man, strive for a distraction-free environment, make friends with those in IT, cut the chit-chat, and, most important, keep your job.

Whether you strive to ultimately become a full-time trader or simply remain in a long-term, part-time trading role in combination with your job, your dreams can be attained. Just make sure you stay the course regardless of how many forks in the road come your way because you have already chosen the path less traveled.

ABOUT THE AUTHOR

Ryan Mallory is the cofounder of SharePlanner.com, which was created to help traders better understand the perplexities of the financial markets and to provide an online community of traders who are able to be honest and transparent in their trading endeavors, as well as develop and master the art and craft of technical analysis.

Ryan has been trading for more than 20 years, after originally getting his start as an eleven-year-old boy under the guidance of his father. Since then, he has grown as a trader and continues to this day using technical analysis to guide his trading strategies.

Prior to fully devoting himself to SharePlanner and full-time trading, Ryan spent a decade in the corporate world, with jobs ranging from Human Resources and law as well as time spent on Capitol Hill and working for a firm as a contracts manager. But nothing ever compared to the thrill of trading stocks, and his hope always was to one day trade full-time for himself, which he was finally able to realize.

Ryan is a graduate of the University of Central Florida with a degree in political science and a minor in economics. He graduated from Nova Southeastern with a master's in business administration.

Ryan is a native central Floridian and still calls it home with his wife and son.

ABOUT THE COMPANION WEBSITE

This book includes a companion web site, which can be found at www.wiley.com/go/pttrader. The site contains *The SharePlanner Trading Guide for The Part-Time Trader*, a valuable resource that will better equip you for the rigors that come with trading part-time and managing a full-time job simultaneously. In his guide, Ryan provides his favorite and most reliable trade setups that you can quickly and easily incorporate into your own trading strategy.

To receive this valuable guide, visit the book's web site at www.wiley.com/go/pttrader. When prompted for a password, please enter "mallory."

INDEX

B

Bollinger bands, 127–128

C

Capital inventory turnover, 130
Chart types, 125–126
Company Wi-Fi, avoiding, 106–108
Corporate depression, 14–15
Corporate hierarchy, 7–10
  "Debbie" employees, 7–8
  "Edward" employees, 7
  "Gary" employees, 8–9
  "Larry" employees, 9
Coworker backlash, xxi–xxii

D

Day job, keeping, 49–64
  avoiding goals that give a false sense of hope, 52–62
    focusing on the trade, 59
    jeopardizing trade vs. job, 62–64
    logic, losing, 53–54
    mind-numbing trading, 56
    real-world fantasies, 56–57
    right position sizes, 60–62
    the squeeze, 58–59
    training class, 57
    unrealistic trading goals, 54–56
    unstoppable trader, 53
  hierarchy, 50–52
    making everyone happy, 51
    managing job and trading, 52
"Debbie" employees, 7–8
Delayed e-mails, 86–87
Deputy program manager, 51

E

"Edward" employees, 7
E-mail paranoia, 13
Escape hatch, finding, 14

F

Finding a way out, 4–6
  real estate, problems with, 5–6
  stocks, 6
Full-time trader, becoming, 17–33
  trading foundation, 18–25
    investing, turning against, 19–21
    new trading world, 19
    open-mindedness, 21–22
    penny stocks, moving beyond, 21–25
    road bumps ahead, 22–24
    rudimentary understanding of risk, 18–19

G

Gaps on first day of trading month, 28
"Gary" employees, 8–9
Group lead, 50
Guest connection, using, 106

H

Head contracts manager, 50

I

Information technology (IT) department, 95–109
  choosing between large and small company, 98–99
    becoming irreplaceable, 98
  employees, getting to know, 99–105
  large companies, 97–98
    blending in, 97
    indiscriminate toward individual performance, 97–98
  small companies, 96–97
    blending in, 96
    doing a good job, 96–97
  understanding their policies and designing trading around them, 105–108
    company apps, installing, 108
    company Wi-Fi, avoiding, 106–108
    guest connection, using, 106
    obstacles, working around, 105
    saving tips, 105–106
Inward reflection, 10–11
IPT manager, 50

J

Job, being successful at, 38–44
  filling out your own review, 41–44
  good Samaritan, 40–41
    peer kindness, 41
    sending a review request, 41
  yearly review, 39–40
    approach, 40
    creating a friendly coalition, 39–40

L

"Larry" employees, 9

M

Management curiosity, xxii
Margin, avoiding use of, 151–153
MBA Holdings (MBAH), 22–23

N

90/10 rule, 143–145

O

Office layout, 67–71, 72
Office routes, 84
Office Space, 35, 49

P

Parameters to account for, 63–64
Parking location, 83–84
Passive income, 123–134
  aiming small, 131
  becoming systematic in trading, 124–128
    Bollinger bands, 127–128
    chart types, 125–126
    price and volume, 126–127
    trend following the markets, 126
  combining the day job with part-time trading, 124
  hitting singles and doubles, 131–134
  risk and reward, being cognizant of, 128–130
    stops, risk in, 128–129
    waiting, 130
Penny stocks, avoiding, 158–159
Position sizes, 137–139
Pre-workday, 81–94
  premarket research, 81–92
    delayed e-mails, 86–87
    Dow Jones Industrial Average, avoiding, 89
    leaving lights on, 87–88
    market analysis, 88–89
    prideful management, 86
    running late, 83–85
    start-time struggles, 82–83
    trade setups, knowing, 89–91
    trading your plan, 91–92
    typical morning, 82

tailoring strategy for the day around workload, 92–94
"prop firms," avoiding, 93–94
trading fallacies, avoiding, 93
Price and volume, 126–127
Professional paper pushers, 2–13
Profits, obsessing over, 29–33
emotions, controlling, 32–33
learning experience, 31
market reality, 30–31
overinvesting, 29–30
risk aversion, understanding, 32
Program contracts manager, 50
Program manager, 51
Project engineer, 51
Project manager, 50–51
Propietary trading firms, avoiding, 93–94

Q

Quitting your job, 193–202
building your own computer, 194–195
employee benefits, giving up, 196
final decision, 193–194
knowing when to leave, 198–200
providing transparency and honesty, 197–198

R

Risk aversion, understanding, 32
Responsibility, seeking out vs. effective trading, 44–47
adversity, overcoming, 46–47
job as a trading asset, 47
offloading, 44–46
broad-based mindset, 45–46
endless competition, 46
increased workload, 45
promotion competition, 45
Risk and reward, being cognizant of, 128–130
stops, risk in, 128–129
"Ryan" employees, 10

S

SharePlanner Investment System, 140–141
Smartphones and tablets, using as trading tools, 77–78
social media and workplace trading, 77–78
StockTwits, 78
Stop-losses, 135–137
Suspicion, avoiding, 111–121
coworkers, 115–119
contrarian indicator, 118–119
mild man trader, 118
humorous stories, 119–121
mouse clicks, 112–114
alternative to, 112–113
monitor privacy, maintaining, 114
taskbar, hiding, 113
social media, 114–115

T

ThinkorSwim trading platform, 33
Time-zone trading, 90–91
Trade setups, notebook of, 90
Trading habits to avoid, 149–159
emotion, 153–155
margin, avoiding use of, 151–153
passion for trading, 155–157
penny stocks, avoiding, 158–159
shortcomings, learning from, 149–151
winning trades turning into losers, 157–158
protecting gains, 157–158
Trading at work, 26–28, 135–145, 161–180
blocking out time, 163–164
boss, confrontation with, 178–180
emotions on the job, 161–162
90/10 rule, 143–145
plan your trade and trade your plan, 141–143
planning around meetings, 162–163
position sizes, 137–139
SharePlanner Investment System, 140–141
sneaking out of meetings, 164–166
bailing out, 165–166
calling in, 165
extreme measures, 164–165
screen share, avoiding, 166
stop-losses, 135–137
trading as a distraction, 171–180
curious coworkers, dealing with, 173–178
traveling, trading and, 166–169
adding new positions prior to, 168
travel time, using, 168–169
workload, using to trading benefit, 169–170

Trend following the markets, 126
Tricks of the trade, 181–191
image and performance, 182–183
learning to do two things at once, 183–184
network tricks, 184–186
bandwidth red flags, 185
guest network, using, 184–185
streaming, using handheld technologies for, 185–186
scaling in and out of positions, 186–187
simple breakdown, 186–187
socializing, 188–189
spreading papers, 189–190
Twitter, 77–78

U

Urologix (ULGX), 19–20

W

West Coast trading, 167–168
Work ambivalence, 36–38
nonsensical reports, 36–37
workplace scalawag, 37–38
Workplace armageddon, 102–104
Workplace trading desk, essentials to, 65–78
assigned computer, 71–72
desktop computer, using, 75–77
upgrades, getting, 75–76
Web-based trading, 76–77
desktop vs. laptop, 72–75
additional advantages of laptop, 75
laptop portability, 73–74
meetings, getting through, 74
request form, filling out, 73
environmental trading, 65–66
office layout, 67–71, 72
office squares, 66
small office, choosing, 66–67
smartphones and tablets, using as trading tools, 77–78
social media and workplace trading, 77–78

Y

Yearly review, 39–40
approach, 40
creating a friendly coalition, 39–40
filling out your own review, 41–44
good Samaritan, 40–41
peer kindness, 41
sending a review request, 41